CARLOS LISCHETTI

ANIMATION
IN SUGAR

DEDICATION

To my Mum and Dad for their unconditional support all through my ups and downs.
Also to Kella Roffo who is always in my heart and thoughts.

First published in September 2012 by B. Dutton Publishing Limited, The Grange, Hones Business Park, Farnham, Surrey, GU9 8BB.
Copyright: Carlos Lischetti 2012

ISBN-13: 978-1-905113-35-4

All rights reserved.

Reprinted in December 2012

No part of this publication may be reproduced, stored in a retrieval system or transmitted in any form or by means electronic, mechanical, photocopying, recording, or otherwise, without prior written permission of the copyright owner. A catalogue record of this book is available from the British Library.

Carlos Lischetti has asserted his right under the Copyright, Designs and Patents Act, 1988, to be identified as the author of this work.

Publisher: Beverley Dutton

Group Editor: Jenny Stewart

Art Director/Designer: Sarah Ryan

Editor: Jenny Royle

Designer: Zena Deakin

Graphic Designer: Louise Pepé

Copy Editor: Amy Norman

Editorial Assistant: Frankie New

PR and Advertising Manager: Natalie Bull

Photography and illustrations: Elio Lischetti

Printed in China

Acknowledgements

I am very grateful to my editors and all the Squires Kitchen team for their hard work and enthusiasm for my book. My gratitude also goes to Beverley and Robert Dutton for giving me the opportunity to publish my book and for their belief in my work.

I have been so fortunate to work with my brother, Elio. His hard work on our book project and his perfectionism, which sometimes drove me crazy, led me on to success. Thanks also to my sister, Mercedes, my dear 'Mechi'. Her birthday always gave me the opportunity to try out a new cake – she was my guinea pig! Te quiero Hermana! By the way… Where is Mauro?!

Special thanks to my Granny Amable, always there ready to listen to my latest news, sharing her constant enthusiasm in everything I did, helping me in the kitchen when I was rushing to deliver a cake. I will never forget the walnut cake the whole family used to make in Máximo Paz! Her baking and cooking inspired me to become what I am today.

I want to mention also all my cousins and uncles who were always ready to have a piece of cake, even the leftovers!

Heartfelt thanks to my good friend and flatmate, Adrian, for his endless patience, unselfish help and never-ending enthusiasm in everything he does. It all means a lot to me.

I owe a debt of gratitude to Omar from the Gelus sugarcraft shop for his initial support during my first steps into sugarcrafting.

Even now I cannot find the right words to thank the lovely Sheila Brown for helping me with corrections for the book. She was at hand when I got into a muddle with words, and especially when I had deadlines to meet.

I have been fortunate to have had the support of so many friends in Argentina and all over the world, including wonderful colleagues from Rosario, with whom I spent really memorable times there teaching in different schools.

Thank you to everyone that I have had the pleasure to work with over past years who helped me to develop my career. These include all the people who believed in me and kept faith even when they had to endure the mistakes I made on the way.

I will always be indebted to Kella Roffo – I spent nine wonderful years working in her bakery in Rosario where this whole story began. She set me on my first steps in pastry-making and treated me just like her own son.

Finally, thanks to my beloved Mum who always kept a close eye on me, checking if my figures looked right and pointing out my mistakes; and deep gratitude and heartfelt thanks to my Dad for always being there and giving me the gift of life. I love you both very much.

Disclaimer

INTRODUCTION

Now that I have written my first book, I feel that I have finally arrived at the moment of truth! After all the years spent baking cakes and then creating my sugar figures, I feel the time is ripe to share my sugar modelling techniques and ideas with other sugarcrafters, as well as with those who are new to the craft.

In writing this book my hope is that it is not only an inspiration to others but also a resource for those who wish to develop their own ideas and techniques. My wish is to encourage and motivate crafters whenever they are challenged to create their own new piece of sugar work.

In this book I have tried to present new ways of modelling which push the boundaries beyond earlier techniques. Part of the process for me was working with my brother, Elio, who is an artist. Elio produced drawings of characters and the challenge for me was to reproduce these in sugar, prompting me to explore new methods of modelling figures. I had to discover a system of making each figure in a way that was as easy as possible and, most importantly, achievable and enjoyable. I was aware that if I could not make it myself then neither could my readers, so I hope that I have achieved this.

Before the cake decorating projects you will find some of my favourite cake recipes which I have used and loved throughout my life. These are the recipes I grew up with and on which I carried out my first experiments in sugarcraft.

I have tried to give you, my readers, the book I would have liked to have to hand when I was learning my craft. It would have saved so much time and heartache! However, I do not regret the experience I have had of learning through my mistakes, of working through them and finally overcoming them.

I am presenting my way of working to you, but always remember that this is not the only way. Use this book as your stepping stone, to be inspired and to find your own way in the wonderful world of sugarcraft.

Carlos

CONTENTS

CELEBRATION CAKES

Essential Edibles and Equipment

Equipment

You will need the same basic items for most of the projects in this book, so it is worth investing in any items that you don't already have. Any specific requirements for either edibles or equipment are listed at the beginning of each cake so make sure you have everything you need before you start a project. All of the items are readily available from sugarcraft suppliers, see page 192.

Cake smoothers (1)

Clear alcohol, e.g. gin or vodka (2)

Cocktail sticks (3)

Cornflour/corn starch/maize starch in a muslin bag (4)

Cutting wheel (5)

Dresden tool (6)

Dried spaghetti

Edible food colours (SK) (7)

Floral wires (8)

Icing/confectioners' sugar (for dusting)

Kitchen paper

Non-slip mat (9)

Non-stick board (10)

Non-toxic glue stick

Paintbrushes for painting, dusting and gluing (SK) (11)

Palette knives, straight and cranked

Plain-bladed knife (12)

Plastic cake dowels

Pliers (13)

Polystyrene base and pieces (to use as support during drying)

Round cutter set (14)

Ruler

Serrated carving knife

SK Black/Brown Professional Food

Colour Pen

SK Confectioners' Glaze

SK Cutting Tool (15)

SK Edible Glue (sugar glue)

Small and large rolling pins (16)

Small, medium and large ball tools (17)

Small parchment paper piping bags (18) (see page 8)

Small scissors (19)

Toothbrush, new (20) (for paint effects, see page 47)

White vegetable fat/shortening (21)

Wooden skewers (22)

How to make a cornflour dusting bag

A dusting bag is always useful for dusting the work surface evenly when you are going to roll out pastillage, flower paste or modelling paste, and can be used to dust your hands to keep them dry when you are modelling. However, when rolling out marzipan or sugarpaste to cover a cake, always use icing sugar rather than cornflour (see pages 34 to 36).

Edibles

1tbsp cornflour/corn starch/maize starch

Equipment

A piece of muslin

Elastic band

1 Cut a piece of muslin into two squares and layer one on top of the other. Place a full tablespoon of cornflour in the centre.

2 Bring the four corners together to create a bag and secure with an elastic band.

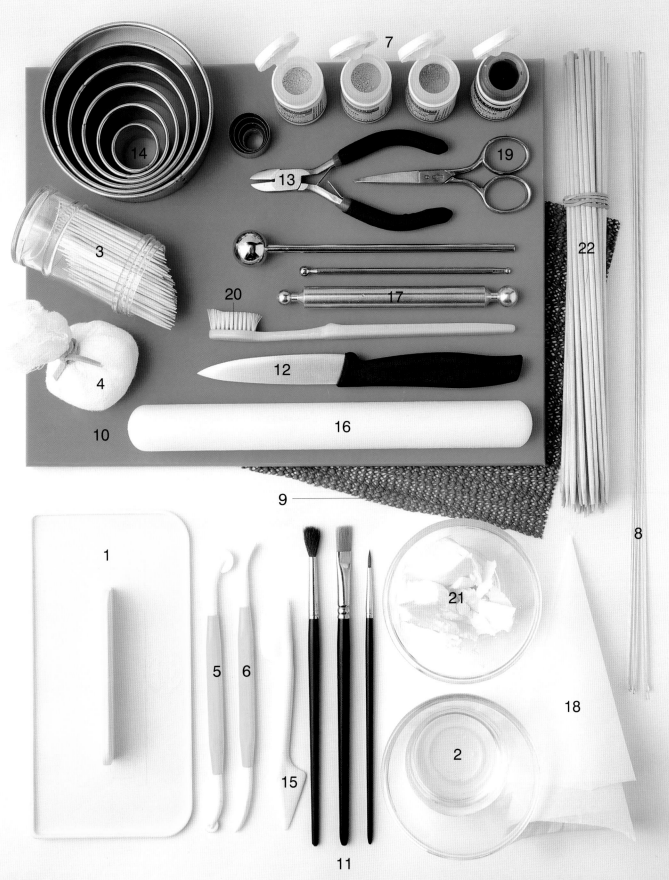

How to make a paper piping bag

Paper piping bags are always useful when only a small amount of royal icing is needed. They are good for piping small amounts of royal icing into eye sockets, sticking pieces of dry pastillage together and piping details such as hair.

Edibles

Royal icing (see page 27)

Equipment

Parchment paper

Scissors

Piping nozzle (optional)

1 Take a triangle of parchment paper and fold it in half to mark the central point on the long side.

2 Bring one side of the triangle round to form a cone shape, ensuring that the point is in the centre of the long side.

3 Holding the first side in place with one hand, bring the other side around to complete the cone.

4 Hold the ends in place, ensuring that the points of the triangle are all at the back of the cone.

5 Fold the points over twice so that the bag holds its shape. If you are using a piping nozzle, snip off the tip of the bag and drop the nozzle into the bag, then half-fill the bag with royal icing. Once the icing is in the bag, squeeze it to the end then fold the top over again to seal the bag ready for piping.

RECIPES

BUTTER SPONGE CAKE

There are many recipes for butter sponge cakes that I personally like; you can try the one suggested here or use your own favourite. This is a classic Victoria sponge recipe that I often use as it gives a spongy consistency and a firm crumb for coating the cake with marzipan or sugarpaste (see pages 34 to 38). This basic recipe for a vanilla-flavoured cake can be changed to chocolate, lemon, orange or walnut by adding extra flavours (see notes on variations opposite).

Ingredients

200g (7oz) softened butter

1tsp natural vanilla essence

200g (7oz) icing or caster sugar (I prefer to use icing sugar as it gives a finer crumb when baked)

200g (7oz) eggs (equivalent to 4 medium free-range eggs)

200g (7oz) self-raising flour or 200g (7oz) plain/all-purpose flour with 2 level tsp baking powder, sifted

Equipment

3 x 15cm (6") shallow round cake tins or rings

Baking parchment

Mixer with paddle attachment

Rubber spatula

Sieve

Wire rack

Cling film

1 Grease and flour three 15cm (6") diameter round cake tins. Line the bottom of each tin with baking parchment if you haven't used the tin much before. Preheat the oven to 170–180°C/350°F/gas mark 4.

2 Cream the butter, vanilla essence and sugar in an electric mixer with the paddle attachment until light and fluffy. Scrape the bowl to make sure there are no lumps of butter stuck to the bottom.

3 Add one egg at a time, mixing well after each addition. (Don't worry if the mix curdles at first, this is normal as the butter can't emulsify properly with the addition of the extra water in the eggs.)

4. Stir in the sifted flour in two batches, mixing at a slow speed.

5. Scrape the sides and bottom of the bowl with a rubber spatula to make sure that all the ingredients are completely mixed and that there are no traces of flour left.

6. Split the mix into three tins and spread out evenly. Place the tins in the middle of the oven and bake for approximately 20 minutes. The cake is ready when it is light brown on top; if you insert a skewer it should come out clean. Another test is to gently press your fingers on the centre of the cake and, if it is done, it should bounce back. If it's still wobbly put it back in the oven for a few minutes until it is completely baked.

7. Once the cakes are baked, turn them onto a wire rack and allow to cool.

8. Once the cake is cold, wrap it in cling film to prevent it from drying out.

Flavourings

Chocolate: replace 50g (1¾oz) of flour with 50g (1¾oz) of a good quality cocoa powder.

Lemon or orange: add the zest of one lemon or one orange when you cream the butter and sugar.

Walnut: add 80g (2¾oz) of chopped walnuts to the flour and fold into the mix.

TUTOR TIPS

The eggs should be at room temperature.

The butter should be soft but not melted. If you live in a warm country, keep the butter in the fridge until it is needed.

I prefer to split and bake the mix in two or three tins rather than in one as it produces an even shape and a lighter crumb. When you overfill the tin, the cake crumb becomes tighter and heavier than it should be.

Always cream the butter with the vanilla essence or the citrus zest to achieve maximum flavour.

Cake mix quantities

The following charts can be used as a reference when baking cakes of different sizes using the butter sponge recipe; the second chart shows the quantities of the recipe used for the cakes in this book. The amount of cake mix given is enough to make a cake that can be split into three before baking. The amount of mix you use in the tins will depend on the height your layer needs to be, but remember not to overfill the tins with the mix or the cake will turn out heavy and doughy. It is better to bake as many layers of cake as needed to achieve the height required.

Tin size (round or square)	Amount of mix for 3 layers	Multiple of recipe
3 x 10cm (4")	400g (14oz)	½
3 x 15cm (6")	800g (1lb 12oz)	1
3 x 20cm (8")	1.2kg (2lb 10oz)	1½
3 x 22cm (9")	1.6kg (3lb 8oz)	2

Project	Cake shapes/sizes	Amount of mix	Multiple of recipe
Ballerina	3 x 20cm (8") round	1.2kg (2lb 10oz)	1½
Bouncing Baby	3 x 15cm (6") round	800g (1lb 12oz)	1
Queen of Hearts	20cm (8") diameter x 14cm (5½") deep skirt shape	1.2kg (2lb 10oz)	1½
Robot	3 x 15cm (6") round	800g (1lb 12oz)	1
Flora the Woodland Fairy	Please refer to the Light Sponge recipe (see page 12)		
The Quest for Food	2 x 35cm x 25cm (14" x 10") trays	2.4kg (5lb 4oz)	3
Fashionista	Please use the chart above to make a cake to the size required.		
Dune Buggy	2 x 15cm x 20cm (6" x 8") trays	1.6kg (3lb 8oz)	2
Granny's Kitchen	9cm (3½") diameter x 11cm (4¼") deep skirt shape	400g (14oz)	½
Penny-farthing	3 x 20cm (8") round	1.2kg (2lb 10oz)	1½
Moulin Rouge	3 x 20cm (8") round	1.2kg (2lb 10oz)	1½
Just Married	3 x 20cm (8") round	1.2kg (2lb 10oz)	1½
Winter Wonderland	12cm (4¾") diameter x 7cm (2¾") deep hemisphere 9cm (3½") diameter x 4cm (1½") deep hemisphere	800g (1lb 12oz) split between the two hemisphere-shaped moulds	1
Santa's on his Way!	15cm (6") round 10cm (4") round 7cm (2¾") round (bake a 10cm (4") cake and cut out with a round cutter)	800g (1lb 12oz) 400g (14oz) 200g (14oz)	1 ½ ¼

LIGHT SPONGE

I use this recipe when using the sponge sheet technique to line the mould when assembling a cake (see page 32). I would always recommend making one small batch of the light sponge recipe at a time. The maximum number of eggs that I use for one batch is eight (double the recipe below), as that fits perfectly into any regular size electric mixer bowl and will still give your sponge a light and airy texture.

Ingredients

4 large eggs, yolks and whites separated (medium free-range eggs)

120g (4¼oz) caster sugar

120g (4¼oz) plain/all-purpose flour, sifted

1tsp vanilla essence

Equipment

40cm x 30cm (16" x 12") baking tray, lined with baking parchment

Whisk

Spatula

Flavouring

Chocolate: replace 30g (1oz) of flour with 30g (1oz) of cocoa powder, then sift together and follow the recipe as for the vanilla sponge.

1   Preheat the oven to 220°C/425°F/ gas mark 7.

2   Whisk the yolks with 60g (2oz) of sugar and the vanilla essence until thick and pale. Set aside.

3   In a separate bowl, whisk the whites until light and fluffy. Incorporate the rest of sugar into the whites while whisking at medium speed, until soft peaks are formed.

4   Fold half of the soft-peak meringue into the yolks. Once they are combined, add the rest.

5   Sift and fold the flour into the mix two or three times using a spatula.

6   Spread the batter evenly on the tray using a palette knife.

7   Bake for six to eight minutes until the surface is light brown and the sponge springs back to the touch. Remove from the oven and leave to cool on the tray. Cover the sponge with cling film to prevent the sponge sheet from drying out.

For Flora the Woodland Fairy, bake one 40cm x 30cm (16" x 12") sheet of cake using the recipe above. When cool, cut the sponge sheet lengthways into three 10cm (4") strips and roll them up into a roulade with your chosen filling (see pages 18 to 23).

Mini orange cakes

Ingredients

For the cake:

200g (7oz) softened butter

200g (7oz) caster sugar

4 eggs

2 egg yolks (medium free-range)

225g (8oz) self-raising flour or 225g (8oz) plain/all-purpose flour with 1½tsp baking powder, sifted

50g (1¾oz) ground almonds

1tsp orange zest

100g (3½oz) diced, candied orange peel

For the syrup:

150g (5oz) sugar

25ml (1fl oz) lemon juice

125ml (4½fl oz) orange juice

50ml (1¾fl oz) orange or lemon liqueur (Cointreau or Limoncello)

For the decoration:

Warm apricot jam (glaze)

500g (1lb 1oz) SK Fondant Icing

SK Liquid Food Colours of your choice (optional)

SK Instant Mix Royal Icing

Equipment

4cm (1½") half-sphere silicone mould tray

Mixer

Plastic piping bag

1cm (³/₈") round piping nozzle

Pastry brush

Bowls

Fork

Piping bag

Scissors

TUTOR TIP

If you live in a warm climate, store the mini fancies in a box in the fridge until you are ready to serve. You can also fill the domes with orange or lemon curd to enhance the citrus flavour of the cake.

1   Preheat the oven to 200°C/400°F/ gas mark 6.

2   Place the butter, caster sugar and orange zest in the bowl of a mixer fitted with the paddle attachment and cream until light and fluffy. Add the eggs and yolks one at a time, mixing well after each addition. Fold in the flour and ground almonds into the batter by hand until thoroughly mixed.

3   To make the mini cake domes (as featured on page 152), place the mixture in a disposable plastic piping bag fitted with a 1cm (3/8") round nozzle and fill the small silicone half-spheres up to 2/3. Bake them for approximately eight to ten minutes (or longer if you are using larger moulds).

4   Remove the mini cakes from the oven and allow them to cool in the silicone mould. Once cold remove each one from the mould and level the base of the dome if required using a serrated

knife. Once levelled, place each cake back into the mould.

5   To make the syrup, combine the sugar, lemon and orange juice in a small pan. Place the pan over medium heat and bring to boil. Let the syrup boil for two minutes then remove from the heat. Pour the liqueur into the syrup and use it while it is still hot. (Make sure the cake is cold before you brush the hot syrup onto it.)

6   Use a clean pastry brush to spread the hot orange syrup over the cake to moisten it (try not to over-soak it). Cover with cling film and chill them in the fridge for a couple of hours.

7   Before coating the mini cakes with liquid fondant, seal the crumb of the cake by brushing warm apricot jam all over the surface of each dome.

8   Place 500g (1lb 1oz) of fondant in a heatproof bowl and dissolve

it over a bain marie or in the microwave. Do not let the fondant boil.

9   If you are using two different colours as shown, divide the fondant into two bowls and colour one in pink and the other with cyclamen until you get the shade desired.

10   Dip the domes upside down into the fondant one at a time, using a fork to lift them once coated. Hold each dome with two fingers at the bottom and place on a wire rack to let the excess fondant drip from the sides. Once the fondant has set, slide a palette knife underneath the domes to release them from the rack. Place each dome into a paper case or onto the presentation plate.

11   To decorate each dome, fill a small paper piping bag with pale pink-coloured royal icing and snip off the very end of the bag. Pipe a swirl on top of each mini cake, starting at the centre.

CAKE POPS

There are many recipes for cake pops but I use this one as it is quite easy to make when you don't have time to bake a sponge cake.

Ingredients

300g (10½oz) crushed digestive biscuits (plain or chocolate)

100g (3½oz) hazelnut spread (Nutella) or *dulce de leche*

250g (8¾oz) white, milk or dark chocolate, tempered

SK Cocol Colour of your choice (optional)

Equipment

Mixing bowl

Spatula

Plastic food-grade gloves

Lollipop sticks

Polystyrene block

1   In a bowl, mix the crushed biscuits plus the filling of your choice by hand with a spatula until they are combined. Add a bit more of the filling if needed to achieve a workable paste consistency.

2   Wearing a pair of food-grade gloves, roll small balls of the mixture in the palms of your hands.

3   Place the balls in the fridge to firm for an hour or so.

4   To prevent the cake pops from sliding down the sticks, first dip one of the lollipop sticks into the tempered chocolate then insert it into the centre of a ball of mixture. The chocolate will set quickly, securing the cake pop to the stick.

5   Dip the cake pops in white, milk or dark tempered chocolate. If you are using white chocolate, you can colour it as required using Cocol chocolate food colouring.

6   Leave the cake pops to dry in a polystyrene block.

VANILLA BISCUITS

This is one of my favourite biscuit recipes because of its crumbly yet firm consistency, which is ideal for decorating with run-out icing. You can store the dough in the freezer for up to two months before baking.

Ingredients

200g (7oz) plain/all-purpose flour

50g (1¾oz) ground almonds

75g (2½oz) caster sugar

100g (3½oz) soft butter

3 egg yolks

Pinch of salt

1tsp of vanilla extract (or the seeds of 1 vanilla pod)

Equipment

Sieve

Mixer with a paddle attachment

Cling film

Biscuit cutters

Baking tray

Baking parchment

1 Sift the flour and the pinch of salt into the bowl of a mixer fitted with the paddle attachment. If you are making chocolate or cinnamon flavour, add the cocoa or cinnamon at this stage.

2 Add the ground almonds and the caster sugar to the bowl and give it a quick stir to combine all the dry ingredients.

3 Add the soft butter and start mixing at a low speed until you get a crumbly consistency, like sand. Pour in the egg yolks, vanilla extract (or seeds) and citrus zest (for a lemon or orange cake) and keep whisking until the dough starts to form. Take care not to over-mix the dough.

4 Take the dough out of the bowl and wrap it in cling film, leaving the dough in a flat square shape. Place the dough in the fridge for at least one hour to firm, or leave overnight.

5 Before cutting the biscuits, knead the dough with the palms of your hands to make it pliable and then roll it out to a thickness of 5mm (just over ⅛") on a work surface dusted with plain flour.

6 Cut out the biscuits with your chosen cutter then set them out on a tray lined with baking parchment. Place the tray in the fridge to chill the biscuits before baking.

7 Bake at 170°C/325°F/gas mark 3 until the biscuits are slightly brown on the top and sides. Baking time will depend on the size of the biscuits, but as a guide, 5cm (2") round biscuits will take approximately 10–12 minutes.

TUTOR TIP

Bake the biscuits until they have an even, golden brown colour; if you leave them too pale they will taste of raw flour.

Flavourings

Chocolate: replace 50g (1¾oz) of flour with 50g (1¾oz) of unsweetened cocoa powder.

Cinnamon: add a heaped teaspoon of ground cinnamon to the recipe.

Lemon or orange: add a heaped teaspoon of citrus zest to the recipe.

Fillings

Meringue buttercream

I use this recipe as a filling and for crumb-coating sponge cakes: the Italian meringue gives a smooth texture and lightness. Remember that the recipe and flavour variations are given as a guide but remember that you can always choose your own favourite recipes to make sure that the cake tastes as good as it looks.

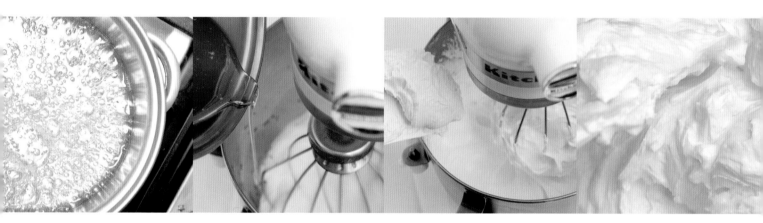

Ingredients

300g (10oz) caster sugar

100ml (3½fl oz) water

150g (5oz) egg whites (equivalent to 4 medium free-range egg whites)

350g (12¼oz) softened butter

Vanilla essence (or any other flavour suggested below)

Equipment

Small saucepan

Digital thermometer (optional, see tip below)

Whisk

1   Reserve a tablespoon of the sugar for the egg whites, then place the rest of the caster sugar and water in a small saucepan over a medium heat and bring to the boil, up to 118°C.

2   Meanwhile, whisk the egg whites at medium speed until they are foamy and soft. Add the tablespoon of caster sugar into the whites and keep whisking at a medium speed until the meringue is firm.

3   Pour a thin stream of syrup into the egg whites while whisking at medium to high speed. Continue to whisk until the meringue cools down to 30°C.

4   Add the softened butter to the Italian meringue in three batches while mixing at medium speed.

5   Add your chosen flavour (see opposite) and use straight away for filling or crumb-coating a cake.

Tutor Tip

Use a thermometer to check the temperature of the syrup. If you don't have one, take a spoonful of syrup and pour it into a glass of cold water: if the syrup forms a soft ball it has reached the temperature required.

Flavourings

Dark chocolate: add 150g (5oz) of melted dark chocolate (50% cocoa solids) at 27°C to 500g (1lb 1oz) of buttercream.

White chocolate buttercream: add 250g (8¾oz) of melted white chocolate at 27°C to 500g (1lb 1oz) buttercream.

Vanilla: open two vanilla pods lengthways and scrape out the seeds with the tip of a knife. Mix the seeds into 500g (1lb 1oz) of buttercream. Add a 10ml (2tsp) of natural vanilla essence to enhance the flavour.

Brandy: add 50g (1¾oz) of brandy to 500g (1lb 1oz) of buttercream.

Coffee: dilute 60g (2oz) of instant coffee granules in 15ml (1tbsp) of hot water and add to 500g (1lb 1oz) of buttercream. A dash of brandy complements the coffee flavour perfectly.

Blueberry (or any homemade jam): add 150g (5oz) of blueberry jam to 500g (1lb 1oz) buttercream.

Lemon: add 150g (5oz) of lemon curd and 50ml (1¾fl oz) of fresh lemon juice to 500g (1lb 1oz) of buttercream. As an optional extra, add the zest from half a lemon or candied lemon peel.

Orange: add 120g (4oz) of candied orange peel to 500g (1lb 1oz) of buttercream. As an optional extra, add 50g (1¾oz) of Cointreau or Grand Marnier to enhance the flavour.

TUTOR TIP

Nowadays there is a wide range of concentrated pastes used in patisserie to flavour ice creams or any sort of cream. These work well with buttercream fillings so try experimenting with your own flavours.

SUGAR SYRUP

Sugar syrup can be brushed over a baked sponge cake with a pastry brush to keep it moist and also to add flavour. It is difficult to say exactly how much syrup needs to be added as every sponge can vary in texture, so when brushing the syrup over the sponge, take into account its thickness and the moistness of the crumb.

Ingredients

250g (8¾oz) caster sugar

250ml (8fl oz) water

25ml (1fl oz) lemon juice (optional)

Equipment

Saucepan

Wooden spoon

Jar or heatproof airtight container

TUTOR TIP

Remember to brush over enough syrup to keep a balanced moisture throughout the cake. Do not add too much sugar syrup as the cake will be too sweet and too soft to hold its shape. Remember that the sponge cake will also take some of the moisture from the filling after a few days in the fridge.

1 Combine all the ingredients in a saucepan and place it over a medium heat. Stir occasionally to make sure that the sugar crystals have dissolved.

2 Let the syrup boil for a minute then remove from the heat.

3 Pour into a clean jar or airtight container and put the lid on while it is still hot to stop the water evaporating. Allow to cool to room temperature before use.

4 Store the jar or airtight container in the fridge for up to a month.

Flavourings

Brandy: add 100ml (3fl oz) of brandy as you remove the pan from the heat.

Orange: boil the ingredients with some fresh orange peel (avoid the white pith as it makes the syrup bitter). Add 50ml (2fl oz) of orange liqueur (Cointreau) when you remove it from the heat and pour the syrup through a sieve into the jar.

Lemon: add lemon zest (avoiding the white pith) to the ingredients and a dash of limoncello once you have removed it from the heat. Pour the syrup through a sieve into the jar.

Vanilla: boil the syrup with two vanilla pods, seeds scraped out. Add a few drops of natural Madagascan vanilla essence to the syrup once it has boiled and remove the pod before using.

Chocolate: add one level tablespoon of cocoa powder and 50ml (1¾fl oz) of brandy to the recipe and bring to boil. Use this chocolate syrup only for chocolate sponges.

DARK CHOCOLATE GANACHE

This is one of my favourite fillings because of its creamy texture and consistency. This recipe can be used as a filling and for crumb-coating cakes.

Ingredients

500g (1lb 1¾oz) SK Dark Belgian Chocolate Couverture

500ml (17fl oz) double cream

50ml (1fl oz) honey

Equipment

Saucepan

Large bowl

Whisk

Spatula

1 Pour the cream and honey into a pan over a medium heat and bring to the boil.

2 Place the couverture chocolate into a large bowl. Remove the pan from the heat and pour the cream and honey mixture onto the chocolate. Whisk from the centre to the sides of the bowl until the ganache has a shiny and smooth texture.

3 Cool the ganache down in the fridge, giving it a stir with a spatula from time to time, until it has a creamy and workable consistency.

Flavouring

Brandy: when the ganache is ready, stir in 100ml (3½fl oz) of brandy or another liqueur of your choice (optional).

TUTOR TIP

If preferred, you can replace the honey with glucose. Either of the two will give the ganache a creamy texture.

RASPBERRY GANACHE

I love this filling as the raspberry purée gives a tangy flavour and extra creaminess. For a delicious combination, layer a chocolate sponge with thin layers of raspberry ganache and homemade raspberry jam. Soak the sponge with sugar syrup flavoured with raspberry liqueur for extra moisture and flavour.

Ingredients

500g (1lb 1¾oz) SK Dark Belgian Chocolate Couverture (50% cocoa solids)

300g (10½oz) raspberry purée

200ml (7fl oz) double cream

50ml (1fl oz) honey

50ml (1fl oz) raspberry liqueur

Equipment

Saucepan

Large bowl

Whisk

Spatula

1 Pour the cream, honey, raspberry liqueur and raspberry purée into a pan and bring to the boil.

2 Place the couverture chocolate into a large bowl. Remove the pan from the heat and pour the mixture onto the chocolate. Whisk from the centre to the sides of the bowl until the ganache has a shiny and smooth texture.

3 Cool the ganache down in the fridge, giving it a stir with a spatula from time to time, until it has a creamy and workable consistency.

PASSION FRUIT GANACHE

I love this filling layered between a lemon or almond sponge soaked with peach-flavoured syrup.

Ingredients

650g (1lb 7oz) SK Milk Belgian Chocolate Couverture

300g (10½oz) passion fruit purée

100ml (3fl oz) double cream

30ml (1fl oz) honey

100g (3½oz) butter

Equipment

Saucepan

Whisk

Large bowl

Cling film

1 Place the passion fruit purée, honey and cream in a pan and bring to the boil.

2 Place the milk chocolate into a large bowl. Remove the pan from the heat and pour the passion fruit mixture onto the chocolate. Whisk to combine and add the butter last. Cover with cling film and leave in the fridge to set overnight.

TUTOR TIP

It is advisable to cover the ganache with cling film before storing in the fridge. This will prevent any unwanted fridge odours from affecting the flavour of the ganache.

MARSHMALLOW

Marshmallow has many uses and is fairly straightforward to make, as long as you have a digital thermometer (or sugar thermometer). It can be coloured with paste or liquid food colours and flavoured to taste, and you can pipe it onto biscuits or use it as a filling.

Ingredients

For the gelatine mix:

75ml (2floz) water

18g (½oz) unflavoured gelatine powder

1tsp vanilla essence

Pinch of salt

For the syrup:

65ml (2fl oz) water

220g (7¾oz) caster sugar

30ml (1fl oz) glucose

80ml (2fl oz) honey

Equipment

Mixer with whisk attachment

Heavy saucepan

Digital thermometer

1 To make the gelatine mix: place the water, salt and vanilla essence in the bowl of the mixer and fit it with the whisk attachment. Sprinkle the gelatine evenly over the water and let it stand for ten minutes until you get a spongy consistency.

2 To make the syrup: combine the water, caster sugar, honey and glucose in a heavy pan. Place the pan over a medium heat and bring to the boil until the temperature reaches 117°C/243°F. Try not to stir the syrup while it is boiling to prevent sugar crystals from forming. Once the syrup reaches 117–118°C/243–244°F, remove the pan from the heat and let the syrup temperature drop to 100°C/212°F.

3 Pour the syrup into the gelatine mix whilst whisking at medium speed. Keep on whisking at medium speed until you get a glossy, thick meringue consistency. Once the marshmallow cools to approximately 40–45°C/104–113°F it is ready to use.

How to make 'snowballs'

1 Fit a plastic piping bag with a 5mm (just over ⅛") round Savoy nozzle and fill with warm marshmallow. Pipe the marshmallow into small hemisphere-shaped silicone moulds as shown. (There is no need to spray the mould with oil or dust it with icing sugar before piping the marshmallow.) As you pipe, leave a domed top in order to create a ball shape.

2 Sprinkle each ball with grated coconut, then insert a plastic lollipop stick through the middle and leave the snowballs to set at room temperature for a couple of hours. The time it takes to set will depend on the climate: leave for longer if it is humid.

3 To release the marshmallow, push the silicone hemisphere from below to lift the ball shape and help loosen the marshmallow from the mould. As marshmallow has a stretchy consistency it won't tear easily when you release it from the mould and will hold its shape. Roll the snowballs in grated coconut while they are still moist, ensuring the coconut covers the surface evenly. If you don't like coconut, sprinkle the top of the marshmallows with icing sugar instead.

ICINGS AND SUGAR PASTES

SUGARPASTE

I usually use ready-made sugarpaste as it saves time and has a consistent and workable consistency, however it is always useful to have a sugarpaste recipe to hand if you like to make your own. Remember that the consistency will change depending on the climate so you may need to adjust the recipe slightly.

Ingredients

120ml (4fl oz) water

20g (¾oz) unflavoured gelatine powder

200g (7oz) glucose syrup

30g (1oz) SK Glycerine*

40g (1½oz) melted vegetable fat

2kg (4lb 6½oz) icing/confectioners' sugar

5ml (1 level tsp) SK CMC Gum

10ml (2tsp) clear vanilla essence

Equipment

Heatproof bowl

Rubber spatula

Whisk

Bain marie

Microwave

Sieve

Sealable food-grade polythene bag

*Avoid using glycerine in extremely humid weather conditions.

1 Pour the water into a heatproof bowl. Sprinkle the gelatine over the water and leave it to soak for about five minutes. Place the bowl over a bain marie (double boiler), making sure the bowl isn't touching the water, and bring the water in the bain marie to a simmer. Stir until the gelatine is completely dissolved and has become transparent.

2 Melt the white vegetable fat in a bain marie or a microwave. While the bowl of gelatine is still over the bain marie, add the melted vegetable fat, glucose, glycerine (if needed) and vanilla essence to the gelatine. Whisk thoroughly until all the ingredients are combined. Remove the bowl from the heat.

3 Sift 500g (1lb 1¾oz) of icing sugar with the CMC and pour this into the gelatine mix. Stir well until all the ingredients are combined. Keep adding more icing sugar until the mixture forms a thick paste.

4 Sprinkle a work surface with icing sugar. Scrape the sugarpaste out of the bowl and knead well with the rest of the icing sugar until the paste becomes pliable and no longer sticks to the work surface.

5 Seal the paste in a food-grade polythene bag when you are not using it to prevent it forming a crust (see notes on storage below).

Colouring and storing sugarpaste

Homemade or shop-bought sugarpaste can be coloured and stored in exactly the same way as for modelling paste. Guidelines can be found on page 26.

MODELLING PASTE

It is important to use a good modelling paste when it comes to making figurines. I prefer to use a paste that contains CMC gum (carboxymethyl cellulose): this not only gives the paste good texture and pliability but also helps it hold its shape. There are many different brands on the market but I would always recommend using a paste that you are familiar with and that you feel comfortable using.

To make the modelling paste used for the figures in this book I usually mix equal amounts of SK Mexican Modelling Paste (MMP) and SK Sugar Florist Paste (SFP) together to achieve a firmer consistency than modelling paste on its own. However if you can't get hold of these pastes or you would prefer to make your own, you can follow the recipe below.

Ingredients

50ml (1¾fl oz) water

7g (½tbsp) unflavoured gelatine powder

50g (1¾oz) egg white, at room temperature (I use SK Fortified Albumen and water to make up the 50g (1¾oz)**

120g (4¼oz) glucose syrup

30g (1oz) melted white vegetable fat

5ml (1tsp) SK Glycerine*

15ml (1tbsp) SK CMC Gum

1kg (2lb¾oz) icing/confectioners' sugar (you may need extra, see note on page 42)

50g (1¾oz) cornflour/corn starch/maize starch

10ml (2tsp) clear vanilla essence

Equipment

Heatproof bowl

Bain marie

Whisk

Sieve

Sealable food-grade polythene bag

1 Place the water in a heatproof bowl. Sprinkle the gelatine over the water and leave it to soak for about five minutes. Place the bowl over a bain marie, making sure the bowl isn't touching the water, and bring the water in the bain marie to a simmer. Stir until the gelatine is completely dissolved and has become transparent.

2 To melt the white vegetable fat use a bain marie (double boiler) or a microwave. While the bowl is still over the bain marie, add the melted vegetable fat, glucose, glycerine (if needed) and flavouring to the gelatine. Whisk thoroughly until all the ingredients are combined. Be careful not to overheat the mixture at this point: never bring the gelatine to the boil.

3 Remove the bowl from the heat and stir in the egg whites or reconstituted albumen. The mixture has

to be warm when the whites go in; they will curdle if the gelatine mix is too hot.

4 Sift 500g (1lb 1¾oz) of icing sugar into a bowl with the CMC and the cornflour and then mix in the gelatine. Keep adding more icing sugar until the mixture forms a thick, sticky paste.

5 At this point take the mixture out of the bowl and knead well with the rest of the icing sugar until the paste becomes pliable and no longer sticks to the work surface.

6 Seal the paste in a food-grade polythene bag when you are not using it to prevent it forming a crust (see notes on storage below).

Basic modelling guidelines and tips for using modelling paste can be found on pages 40 to 42.

*Avoid using glycerine in extremely humid weather conditions.

**The Food Standards Agency recommends using only pasteurised egg in any food that will not be cooked (or only lightly cooked).

If you decide to use fresh egg white always use eggs bearing the Lion mark, which guarantees that they have been produced to the highest standards of food safety. All Lion Quality eggs come from British hens vaccinated against salmonella, are fully traceable and have a 'best before' date on the shell as a guarantee of freshness. This is particularly important for cake makers and decorators as you may well use eggs for baking and preparing icings, marzipans and cake fillings.

COLOURING SUGARPASTE AND MODELLING PASTE

A wide range of paste, liquid and dust food colourings is available from sugarcraft suppliers (see page 192), so you can be as creative as you like with your sugar models. Squires Kitchen makes a wide range of food colours which do not contain glycerine so won't affect the consistency of your paste when dry (see page 46).

I recommend using paste food colours to achieve both light and dark hues; liquid food colours can be used for pastel tones only where a small amount of colour needs to be added, but should not be used if you want to achieve an intense colour as adding too much of it will make the paste too soft and sticky.

Paste food colours are concentrated, so only add a tiny amount of colour at a time using the tip of a cocktail stick until the desired colour is achieved. Blend the colour into the paste by kneading well. Let the paste rest in an airtight, food-grade polythene bag for a couple of hours to allow the colour to develop.

How to colour a large amount of sugarpaste (e.g. when covering a cake):

First take a small piece of sugarpaste and add colour to it using the tip of a cocktail stick until a high intensity of the desired hue is produced, e.g. deep red.

Gradually add small portions of this intensely coloured piece of paste into the large amount of sugarpaste until you achieve your chosen colour, e.g. deep red added to white sugarpaste will create a light pink (rose).

This method makes the colour easier to blend and allows for more gradual colouring, meaning that you are less likely to ruin it by adding too much colour straight from the pot to a large amount of white paste.

How to store sugarpaste, modelling paste and pastillage

Once the paste is coloured as required and ready to use, rub the surface with vegetable fat to prevent the paste from forming a crust and leave it to rest in an airtight food-grade polythene bag. Store the sealed bag of paste in a plastic container to keep it moist for longer.

Once it is sealed, homemade sugarpaste, modelling paste and pastillage can be kept as follows:

- At room temperature for up to 15 days.
- In the fridge for up to a month.
- In the freezer for up to two months.

Take the paste out of the fridge or freezer and allow it to reach room temperature. Knead the paste well to achieve pliability before use.

If you are using ready-made pastes, check the pack for storage guidelines.

TUTOR TIP

Do not wrap sugarpaste in cling film as it is slightly porous and therefore doesn't stop the paste from getting a crust.

Royal icing

Royal icing is one of the most basic recipes in cake decorating yet is so useful for its endless possibilities when decorating cakes. I have used Instant Mix Royal Icing from Squires Kitchen throughout the book, but if you prefer to make your own I would recommend the following recipe. Make sure all the bowls and spatulas used for making royal icing are completely clean and grease-free before you start, otherwise the icing will not mix properly.

Ingredients

40g (1½oz) egg white, at room temperature (I use SK Fortified Albumen and water to make up 40g (1½oz) following instructions on the pack)**

250g–300g (8¾oz–10½oz) icing/confectioners' sugar (depending on the size of the egg white)

5ml (1tsp) strained fresh lemon juice

Equipment

Mixer with paddle attachment

Rubber spatula

Airtight plastic container

Cling film

Kitchen paper

**See guidelines on page 25 regarding the use of egg in food that will not be cooked.

1 Place the egg whites in an electric mixer fitted with a paddle attachment. Beat the whites at a medium speed to break them slightly. If you are using dried albumen powder, follow the instructions on the pack to reconstitute it and beat as explained above.

2 Spoon the sifted icing sugar into the egg whites (or reconstituted albumen) while mixing at slow speed. Mix until they have turned creamy, then add the lemon juice. Add more icing sugar until the icing reaches a soft-peak consistency.

3 Place the royal icing in an airtight plastic container and cover it with cling film before sealing the lid to prevent it from drying out. A damp piece of kitchen paper can be placed on top of the film to keep it moist.

Consistencies

You will need varying consistencies of royal icing depending on how you wish to use it:

Soft peaks: to fill eye sockets and draw lines, dots and borders on cakes. Make the icing following the recipe above and check that it forms bent peaks when lifted with a palette knife.

Stiff peaks: for sticking figurines onto a cake and for piping hair. Add a little sieved icing sugar to soft-peak royal icing and re-beat until it forms stiff peaks.

Run-out consistency: for filling spaces between piped lines or for coating cakes and cupcakes. Add

Run-out consistency

Soft peaks

Stiff peaks

a few drops of cold, pre-boiled water from the fridge to make the icing runny. When cut through with a palette knife the icing should settle back in around ten seconds.

TUTOR TIP

Fresh egg whites can be kept in a jar in the fridge for up to 15 days. Some of the water in the whites will evaporate: this will strengthen the egg whites and make them more suitable for use in royal icing.

Colouring royal icing

Colour royal icing with paste or liquid food colours. If you are using paste colours, dip a cocktail stick into the pot, transfer the colour to a bowl of icing and mix in with a palette knife. Add a little food colour at a time until you have achieved the colour you require. For liquid colours use the point of a knife or a pipette to add droplets of colour into the icing and mix well as before.

Once you have coloured the icing, keep the bowl covered with cling film and a damp kitchen towel to prevent the icing from forming a crust.

How to store royal icing

Royal icing can be stored in the fridge for up to a week if you are using fresh eggs. After a couple of days in the fridge you may find that the icing has separated with a thick layer of sugar on the top and a watery consistency underneath. To fix this, take the royal icing out of the fridge and let it come to room temperature. Take it out of the container, making sure that you do not scrape any dry icing from the sides into the mixture. Re-beat it in the mixer until you achieve the original consistency.

PASTILLAGE

The quickest and easiest product to use when making pastillage is SK Instant Mix Pastillage.
As well as being easy to make you are also guaranteed the same consistency every time.
However, if I ever need to make my own pastillage, I always use the following recipe.

Ingredients

80g (2¾oz) egg whites, at room temperature (I use SK Fortified Albumen and water to make up the 80g (2¾oz) following instructions on the pack)**

800g (1lb 12oz) icing/confectioners' sugar, plus extra if needed (see tip below)

5ml (1tsp) SK CMC Gum

Clear vanilla essence

Melted white vegetable fat

Equipment

2 large mixing bowls

Wooden spoon

Sealable food-grade plastic bags

**See note on page 25 regarding the use of egg in food that will not be cooked.

1 Place the egg whites into a large bowl.

2 In another bowl sift half the icing sugar with the CMC gum then pour this into the bowl of egg whites. Mix with a wooden spoon until you get a soft, stretchy dough.

3 At this point take the dough out of the bowl and knead it on a clean work surface with the rest of the icing sugar until it is pliable and no longer sticks to the work surface.

4 Rub the surface of the pastillage with a little melted vegetable fat to prevent it from forming a crust. Store in an airtight food-grade plastic bag. Do not leave pastillage unwrapped as it dries very quickly.

TUTOR TIPS

Bear in mind that the amount of sugar given in the recipes is only a guide. You may need to add extra icing sugar depending on the type of sugar you are using and the weather conditions (e.g. add more icing sugar in humid climates).

Do not roll out too much pastillage at a time as it dries quickly; aim to roll out just enough for the size of the template you are using.

For curved shapes such as cylinders it is best to use pastillage that contains CMC or gum tragacanth. The gum will give extra strength to the paste and will allow it to be wrapped around the former without losing its shape.

TUTOR TIP

Using spacers of the required depth is the best way to achieve an even thickness when rolling out paste. I usually find the following sizes useful: 2mm, 3mm, 4mm, 5mm, 1cm and 1.5cm ($1/16$", $1/8$", just over $1/8$", $3/16$", $3/8$" and $9/16$"). To achieve a greater thickness such as 3cm ($1^3/16$") you can stack them on top of each other. You will find different spacers available from sugarcraft and chocolate suppliers (see page 192).

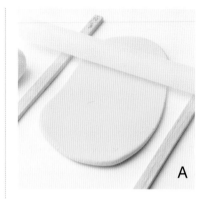

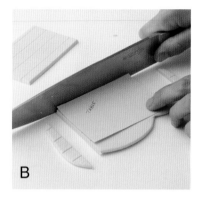

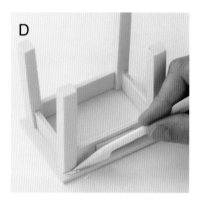

How to use pastillage

1 Roll out some pastillage on a work surface dusted with cornflour. To achieve an even thickness you may find it easiest to use marzipan spacers (picture A).

2 Transfer the pastillage to a chopping board dusted with cornflour, texture if needed and cut out the shape required using a template. Use a sharp, plain-bladed knife to make a neat, straight edge (picture B). To cut circles use a round cutter dusted with a little cornflour.

3 Remove the excess paste from around the edge and leave the piece of pastillage to dry on the chopping board. Flip the piece of pastillage over once it is dry on one side to allow it to dry evenly on both sides. Drying time will depend on the thickness and size of the piece of pastillage and the weather conditions (if conditions are humid it will take longer to dry).

How to stick pieces of dry pastillage together

1 Fill a paper piping bag with soft-peak royal icing, snip off the very end and pipe a line of icing onto the side of the shape that is to be glued in place (picture C).

2 Place the piece in the required position and remove the excess royal icing with the pointed end of a modelling tool or a clean paintbrush (picture D).

3 Once all the pieces are assembled, leave to dry completely.

How to make cylinders from pastillage

1 To make a cylinder shape you will need a plastic tube or a polystyrene cylinder to use as a former. Cut a strip of pastillage using a paper template: the length of the strip must be the same as the circumference of the former.

2 Dust the cylinder with cornflour and wrap the strip around it. Trim the excess paste to make a neat join.

3 Brush one end with a little edible glue and stick the two ends together. Allow to dry.

EDIBLE (SUGAR) GLUE

Edible glue is available to buy from sugarcraft suppliers, however if you would like to make your own, mix one level teaspoon of CMC gum with 150ml (5fl oz) of cooled, boiled water and a few drops of white vinegar. Let the mix rest for a couple of minutes until it becomes gel-like. If you need to adjust the consistency add extra water to make it runnier, or more CMC to make it thicker.

Edible glue can be stored in a jar with a lid and kept in the fridge for up to a month.

Colouring pastillage

Pastillage can be coloured like any other paste (see page 26) but you should bear in mind that extra colour has to be added as it will lighten as it dries. When pastillage pieces are fully dry they can be painted using liquid food colours, edible metallic paint or metallic dust food colours diluted with a few drops of clear alcohol.

How to use edible glue

Edible glue is used for sticking pieces of fresh paste together. The glue will only work if one or both of the modelled pieces is still soft, so stick them together before they dry completely.

Use a paintbrush to dab a small amount of edible glue on the surface and remove the excess with your finger so that you are left with a sticky surface. Do not use too much glue otherwise the pieces may slide out of place.

TUTOR TIP

To make strong edible glue for sticking pieces of dry paste together, mix edible glue with a small amount of pastillage or SFP to form a creamy, tacky consistency.

PREPARING AND COVERING CAKES FOR DECORATION

HOW TO LINE A CAKE WITH A SPONGE SHEET

Lining a cake with a sponge sheet is a technique that I use regularly when layering a large round or square sponge cake with any soft or creamy filling. This technique allows you to get a clean, neat finish on the edge and sides of the cake once it is covered with sugarpaste, and also gives you the option to omit the marzipan covering which is not always to everyone's taste.

If you would prefer to prepare the cake in the traditional way there is no need to bake the sponge sheet to line the cake. Likewise if you are making a small cake you won't need the sponge sheet around the outside to keep its shape, so simply spread the top and sides with a thin layer of buttercream from step 9 overleaf.

Please note that the quantities given are for a 20cm (8") round or square cake.

Edibles

40cm x 30cm (16" x 12") vanilla sponge sheet (see recipe on page 12)*

3 x 20cm (8") round or square sponge cake layers (see pages 9 to 11)

300ml (10½fl oz) sugar syrup (see page 20)

300g (10½oz) filling, e.g. ganache (see pages 18 to 23)

150g (5¼oz) ganache or buttercream for the crumb coat

Equipment

Acetate sheet

20cm (8") round or square cake tin for lining the cake

Paintbrush (sugarcraft use only) or pastry brush

20cm (8") cake card

28cm (11") round cake drum or stainless steel tray to use as base for crumb coating the cake

Cling film

Palette knife

Plastic scraper

Turntable

*One sponge sheet cut lengthways into three strips allows you to line two 20cm (8") round or square tins, approximately 10cm (4") in height.

1 Line the tin or ring used for baking the cake with a strip of acetate of the height required. For a square cake with straight corners, cut the acetate into four pieces and stick them to the inner sides of the tin with a dab of filling.

2 Place a strip of the vanilla sponge sheet all the way around the inside of the tin with the brown crust facing inwards. For a square shape with straight corners, cut the sponge into four pieces, then place and stick them to the acetate sheet with a dab of filling.

3 Place a layer of vanilla sponge at the bottom and brush with sugar syrup. Trim the sides of the sponge layer slightly to fit in the shape if required.

4 Spread a layer of your chosen filling on top and onto the sides of the sponge sheet lining the cake.

5 Repeat the layering process until you reach the height required.

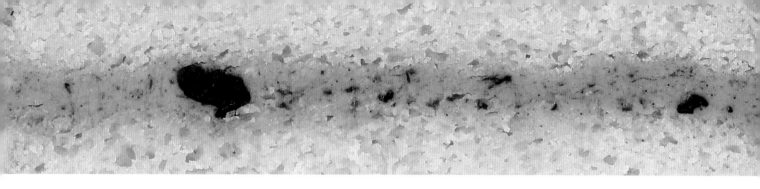

6 Finish the cake with a layer of sponge on the top and brush with syrup.

7 Stick a cake card onto the top layer of sponge with a dab of the filling and wrap the cake in cling film. Store in the fridge until needed.

TUTOR TIP

I recommend that you layer the cake with the filling three days before you decorate it. The cake will mature in flavour and will be evenly moist.

8 Flip the cake over onto the cake drum to release it from the tin. Remove the acetate carefully.

9 To crumb-coat the cake, use a palette knife to spread a layer of buttercream onto the top and sides of the cake. This seals the cake and gives an even surface for the sugarpaste or marzipan to stick to.

10 Remove the excess buttercream with a plastic side scraper: the easiest way to do this is to place the cake onto a turntable and rotate the cake whilst holding the scraper against the side of the cake.

11 Chill the cake for a few hours to allow the buttercream to firm. If you leave the cake overnight make sure you cover it with cling film to protect it from any unwanted fridge odours. Before coating the cake, apply another thin layer of buttercream to help the sugarpaste stick.

TUTOR TIP

You can crumb-coat the sponge cake (already lined with a sponge sheet) with a thin layer of apricot jam instead of using buttercream if preferred.

COVERING A ROUND-EDGED CAKE WITH SUGARPASTE

Most of the cakes in this book are covered with sugarpaste following the method below. The quantity of sugarpaste required for each cake is given at the beginning of each project.

Edibles

Cake, filled and crumb-coated
(see above)
Sugarpaste
Icing/confectioners' sugar in shaker

Equipment

Large rolling pin
Plain-bladed knife
Cake smoothers

1 Remove the crumb-coated cake from the fridge. Take enough sugarpaste to cover your cake and knead until it is soft and pliable.

2 Roll out the sugarpaste on a work surface dusted with icing sugar to a thickness of approximately 5mm (just over 1/8") then lift the paste with the rolling pin and place it gently onto the cake.

3 Use the palms of your hands to smooth the paste across the top and down the sides of the cake in order to stick the paste down and remove any air bubbles. Trim the excess paste from around the base with a plain-bladed knife. When covering round mini cakes, trim the excess paste from around the base using a round cutter.

4 Rub the cake gently with a smoother in each hand to remove any imperfections and to achieve a neat finish.

5 The covered cake is now ready to decorate as required.

COVERING A STRAIGHT-EDGED CAKE WITH MARZIPAN

If you require a cake with a sharp top edge, a marzipan layer will help to create straight edges underneath the sugarpaste coating.

Edibles

Cake, filled and crumb-coated (see above)

Marzipan

Icing/confectioners' sugar in shaker

Sugarpaste

Clear alcohol (e.g. gin or vodka)

Equipment

Large rolling pin

Large cake drum/board (bigger than the cake size)

Plain-bladed knife

Greaseproof paper

Cake smoothers

Cake card the same size as the cake

Pastry brush

1 Remove the crumb-coated cake from the fridge.

2 Roll out some marzipan on a work surface dusted with icing sugar to a thickness of approximately 3mm (1/8"). Transfer the rolled marzipan to a cake board (that is bigger than the cake to be coated) dusted with icing sugar. Place the cake upside down onto the marzipan and trim to size around the bottom edge using a plain-bladed knife.

3 To cover the side of the cake, cut a strip of greaseproof paper to the same height and circumference as the cake. Roll out a piece of marzipan and use the paper template to cut it to the required height and length. Roll up the marzipan strip and stick it to the side of the cake. Unroll the paste around the cake and trim away the excess marzipan neatly at the join.

4 Using two smoothers, press the sides down gently to achieve an even surface and create a neat, straight edge at the bottom.

5 Stick a cake card the size of the cake on top of the cake with a little buttercream and flip the cake back over. Leave the marzipan to firm up before covering with sugarpaste.

6 Dampen the surface of the marzipan with clear alcohol using a pastry brush and cover the cake with sugarpaste as described on page 34.

TUTOR TIP

I like to use marzipan because it gives a nice shape to the cake and keeps it moist. However, if you don't like marzipan you can omit this stage completely, or replace the marzipan with sugarpaste.

COVERING A CAKE BOARD/DRUM WITH SUGARPASTE

To give your cakes a professional finish, place them on a cake board or drum covered with sugarpaste and edged with ribbon.

Edibles

Edible glue

Sugarpaste

Icing/confectioners' sugar in shaker

Equipment

Large paintbrush (sugarcraft use only)

Rolling pin

Cake board/drum

Sharp knife

Ribbon

Non-toxic glue stick

1 Brush the surface of the cake board with a little edible glue.

2 Knead the required quantity of sugarpaste until it becomes pliable. Roll out the paste on a work surface dusted with icing sugar to a thickness of approximately 4mm ($^1/_8$") and to the size of the board that you need to cover. Fold the paste over the rolling pin and place it gently on the board.

3 Rub a smoother over the surface to stick the paste to the board and remove any imperfections.

4 Trim away the excess paste from around the edge using a sharp knife.

5 Secure a length of ribbon onto the edge of the board with a non-toxic glue stick, taking care to ensure that the glue does not come into contact with the sugarpaste. Make a slight overlap at the join then position this at the back when you place your cake onto the board.

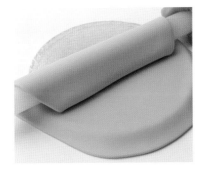

DOWELLING A CAKE

If you are making a stacked cake with more than one tier you will need to dowel the lower tiers to prevent the cake from sinking.

Edibles

Cakes, prepared and covered with sugarpaste, placed on cake cards of the same size

Clear alcohol (e.g. gin or vodka) or boiling water

SK Food Colour Pen (any colour)

Royal icing or watered-down sugarpaste (to secure the cakes together)

Equipment

Dowelling template

Plastic cake dowels

Craft knife

1 Place each cake onto a thin cake card, usually of the same size so it cannot be seen, and cover in the usual way (see page 34).

2 Using a dowelling template or your own template made from greaseproof paper, mark where you would like the dowels to go. Use three dowels for smaller cakes and four for larger cakes so that they have enough support. They should be equally spaced around the central point but within the size and shape of the tier above.

3 Sterilise all the plastic dowels before use by wiping them with clear alcohol or submerging them in boiling water. Allow to dry before use.

4 Push a dowel down into the cake until it touches the board at the base. Mark the dowel level with the surface of the sugarpaste using an edible pen. Repeat with the other dowels in the same tier then remove them and cut them to size using a craft knife.

TUTOR TIP

If the height of the marks on the dowels differs, cut them all to the height of the tallest mark to ensure that the stacked tiers remain level.

5 Insert the dowels back into the cake. When you have dowelled all the upper tiers (except the top one), carefully stack them, using a little watered-down sugarpaste or royal icing to stick them together.

COVERING A DUMMY CAKE

Polystyrene dummy cakes are extremely useful in modelling: I often use them to support cake-top figures as they are firmer than a real cake and, because they are light, they can be placed on top of a cake without the need for cake dowels underneath (unless the cake-top figures are particularly heavy). They are readily available from sugarcraft suppliers (see page 192).

Polystyrene shapes have several other useful purposes in modelling: they are used as supports whilst making figurines; can be covered with sugarpaste to make parts of a figure lighter (such as the sphere shape in the robot torso on page 76); used as a base to transport figurines on; and can be used as formers for pastillage pieces. To cover a polystyrene dummy cake, brush it with edible glue then cover with sugarpaste in the same way as for a real cake (see page 34).

MAKING AND COVERING ROUND MINI CAKES

Edibles

3 quantities of butter sponge cake recipe, flavoured as desired (see page 9)

400ml (14fl oz) sugar syrup (see page 20)

600g (1lb 5¼oz) dark chocolate ganache (see page 21)

600g (1lb 5¼oz) buttercream or ganache for crumb coat (see pages 18 to 21)

2kg (4lb 6½oz) sugarpaste

Equipment

2 baking trays, 35cm x 25cm (14" x 10")

Baking parchment

Cooling rack

7cm (2¾") round cutter

Pastry brush

Piping bag fitted with 1cm (³/₈") round nozzle

Cranked palette knife

12 cake cards, 7cm (2¾") round

Cling film

Makes twelve x 7cm (2¾") round mini cakes.

1 Bake the butter sponge in two trays lined with baking parchment following the recipe on page 9. Flip the cakes onto a wire rack to cool down, wrap in cling film and allow to chill in the fridge overnight.

2 Level the top of the cake with a serrated knife and cut out 7cm (2¾") circles using a cutter. Place the round layers of sponge on a tray lined with baking parchment and use a pastry brush to soak each sponge with sugar syrup.

3 Pipe dark chocolate ganache onto each sponge and place another layer of sponge on top. Brush again with sugar syrup and leave the filling to set in the fridge.

4 Spread a layer of buttercream over the top and sides to seal the crumb, then create an even surface using a cranked palette knife. Stick the mini cake onto a cake card of the same size with a dot of the filling.

5 Keep the mini cakes in the fridge wrapped in cling film to avoid any unwanted fridge odour which may affect the taste.

6 Cover with sugarpaste in the same way as for a large cake (see page 34).

TUTOR TIP

Working on several cakes at once, as if you are on a production line, is always the best way to save time when you are making mini cakes.

MODELLING TIPS AND TECHNIQUES

MODELLING BASIC SHAPES

Making your figurines smooth and crack-free can be difficult if you are not used to modelling. Always make sure you use the right modelling paste (see page 25) and follow these guidelines to make sure your models have a smooth, professional finish.

Ball

Take a piece of modelling paste between your fingers and thumbs and start to stretch and fold the paste to give it a soft and pliable consistency (pictures A and B).

Hold the paste between the palms of your hands and press firmly. Simultaneously squeeze and roll the paste in circular movements in order to smooth out any cracks on the surface of the paste (pictures C and D). Release the pressure but keep moving your hands in a circular motion until you get a smooth ball shape (pictures E and F).

The ball is the most important basic shape to master as, when you start to model, every other shape will emerge from this first ball shape.

Rounded cone/teardrop

Roll a smooth ball then open out your hands as shown and roll the ball up and down to create a pointed end (pictures G and H).

Pear shape

Roll a smooth ball and place it in the palm of one hand. Press and roll the side of your other hand up and down on one half of the ball to create a neck shape (pictures I and J).

TIPS FOR USING MODELLING PASTE

• Rub a little white vegetable fat into the palms of your hands to prevent the paste from sticking to your hands.

• If the paste is sticky you can either knead a little extra icing sugar or a pinch of CMC to the paste to adjust its consistency, especially when the piece needs to be strong.

• If the paste is too hard, knead in a little vegetable fat to make it pliable and stretchy again. A few drops of pre-boiled water can also be added to replenish lost moisture.

• If the paste has developed a dry outer crust, just peel it off with a sharp knife so that you can save the moist piece inside. This usually happens when the paste has not been stored properly in an airtight food-grade plastic bag.

• Keep the paste in the fridge when you are not using it, always sealed in a food-grade plastic bag. This is particularly important if you live in a hot and humid climate.

• If the paste seems too soft and doesn't hold its shape, add pinches of CMC to it until you achieve a firmer consistency.

• In extremely humid weather conditions do not use any paste or food colours that contain glycerine (also known as glycerol). Glycerine absorbs the moisture in the air and will prevent the paste from drying properly.

• If you find that the paste dries quickly whilst you are modelling, add a paste that contains glycerine, such as sugarpaste/rolled fondant which is usually used for covering cakes. The glycerine in the sugarpaste will help the paste to retain moisture for longer.

• The best way to find out how the paste works in specific weather conditions and individual cases is to use it. Trial and error will allow you to make the best decisions when using the paste, so allow plenty of time to practise.

PROPORTIONS FOR CUTE CHARACTERS

When modelling characters the proportions of the figurines affect whether they look cute (larger head) or more realistic (smaller head).

If you make the head (A) roughly the same size as the torso (B) you will end up with a cute-looking character: this basic rule applies to most of the figures modelled in this book. You can vary this head:torso ratio if you want to create a specific type of figure, but the volume of both the head and the torso should be roughly the same if you want to create cute human or animal characters.

From the drawing you can see how I would create a male character with the head the same size as the torso. For a female figure, simply make the waist thinner and add breasts.

When creating a human-like character, take the modelled head or torso as a unit of measurement to help you define the length of limbs, as well as the overall height of the figure. A good height for a human-like character is five or six heads high. The legs are two-and-a-half heads long. Finally, note that the arms should fall slightly higher than the knees when they are attached.

As well as experimenting with different head:torso ratios you can make the legs, arms or neck longer to stylize the character. It is important that you take these proportions as a guide only and do not feel constrained by them

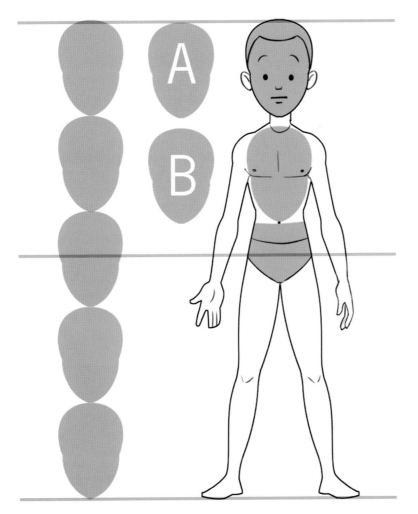

when creating your own figures. I would always encourage you to discover your own cute proportions for modelling and to use the ones I have suggested only as a starting point.

You can portray different ages simply by moving the eyes. Once you have made the head draw an imaginary line across the middle of the face. To make a young person place the eyes below this line and for an older character place the eyes on or above the line. As a rule the lower the eyes are from the middle line the younger the character looks; the higher they are above the line the older the character looks.

The eyebrows are part of an imaginary circle that sits around the eye: this imaginary circle can be stretched or squashed to achieve different expressions as shown below.

Finally, the height of the ears should be between the eyes and the base of the nose.

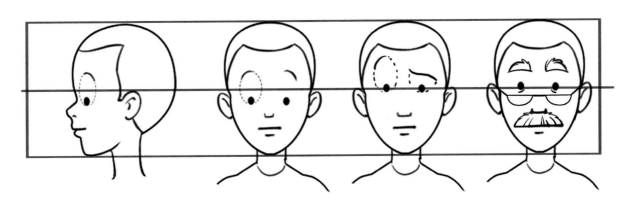

CASTING A SILICONE HEAD MOULD

Sugarcraft suppliers stock several head moulds in different sizes for making sugar figurines: the Great Impressions range from Squires Kitchen includes all the moulds you will need for this book (see page 192). If you are looking to make a head in a different size you can also make your own: with this technique you can create a mould from any doll's head. I like to make my own moulds so that I have different sized heads and expressions for human-like figurines.

Equipment

Silicone moulding paste (e.g. Siligum)

Doll's head, sterilised with clear alcohol

Plaster of Paris

100ml (3½fl oz) cold water

Small plastic container

1 To make the impression of the face, mix the two parts of silicone moulding paste following the instructions on the packet. Make a ball and press it gently onto the doll's face using the heel of your hand to fill in the shape of the face. Leave the silicone paste to set.

2 Meanwhile, make the plaster base that will support the silicone mould. Add teaspoons of plaster of Paris powder to 100ml (3½fl oz) of water, one at a time until you get a thick consistency.

3 Pour the plaster mix into a plastic container that is big enough to hold the head.

4 Gently press the head with the silicone layer into the plaster base and leave it to dry until it has set hard.

5 Once the plaster base has set, remove the doll's head from the silicone mould. Make sure you sterilise the mould before each use with clear alcohol using a piece of kitchen paper.

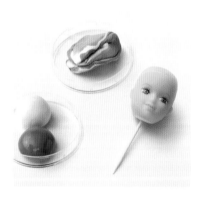

MAKING A HEAD FROM A CAST MOULD

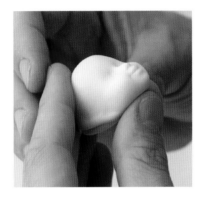

TUTOR TIP

Do not use soft modelling paste when making a head from a mould: firm paste will achieve the best results. For extra strength, add a pinch of CMC to the paste or mix it with an equal amount of SFP for extra strength (see page 25).

1 Roll some modelling paste into a ball and press firmly using your thumb to fill in the shape.

2 Roll some more modelling paste into a ball to fill in the socket created by your thumb.

3 Trim the excess paste with a pair of scissors to shape the back of the head.

4 Insert a cocktail stick into the paste to help you remove it from the mould.

5 Pull the head carefully out of the mould then remove the cocktail stick.

6 Cut away any excess paste from around the edge of the face.

7 Shape the head and add the facial details while the paste is still fresh. Leave to set.

USE OF COLOUR

I have used SK Professional Paste Food Colours to create all of the projects in this book as their range covers the complete colour wheel. If you are not familiar with the range or you are using a different brand you can use the list below to find out how to mix generic colours to achieve your desired colour.

SK Colours	Generic Colours
Poppy	Red + a touch of yellow or orange
Poinsettia	Red + a touch of blue or violet
Rose	Pink
Fuchsia	Pink + a touch of violet
Cyclamen	Red + a touch of lilac or violet
Lilac	Lilac
Terracotta	Red + green or brown
Sunny Lime	Yellow + a touch of green
Berberis	Orange
Daffodil	Yellow
Sunflower	Yellow + a touch of red or orange
Mint	Green
Vine	Green + a touch of yellow
Dark Forest	Green + a touch of red or orange + a touch of blue

SK Colours	Generic Colours
Holly/Ivy	Green + a touch of red or orange
Olive	Green + a touch of yellow + a touch of orange
Cream	White + a touch of yellow + a touch of brown
Edelweiss	White
Jet Black	Black
Teddy Bear Brown	Brown + a touch of yellow
Bulrush	Dark brown
Hydrangea	Green + a touch of blue
Bluegrass	Green + a touch of blue + a touch of yellow
Hyacinth	A touch of blue
Gentian	Blue
Bluebell, Wisteria	Blue + a touch of violet
Plum, Thrift, Violet	Violet

A soft beige skin colour can be made using any of the following options:

SK Colours: white paste + a touch of Teddy Bear Brown or Chestnut
Generic Colours: white paste + a touch of brown + a touch of yellow

or

SK Colours: white paste + a touch of Poppy + a touch of Sunflower
Generic Colours: white sugarpaste + a touch of yellow + a touch of red

Guidelines for colouring modelling paste, pastillage and royal icing can be found on pages 26 to 31.

PAINTING AND COLOURING TECHNIQUES

The different effects that can be created using edible colours are endless. A few of the techniques that I've used in this book are described here: these can be used on virtually any sugar piece to really bring it to life.

Airbrushing

If you have an airbrush you need to use liquid food colours with it. If the colour is too bright, just add a few drops of cooled, boiled water to dilute it. Place the piece to be sprayed over a spare piece of paper and airbrush from a distance to prevent patchiness. Apply a thin layer of colour at a time until you achieve the shade you require. Always start with soft colours and add more layers to build up darker colours. If you do not have an airbrush, similar subtle effects can be created by dusting colour onto the surface of your work (see below).

Splashing technique

I love using this technique as you don't need to have an airbrush. Dilute some liquid or paste food colour with several drops of cooled, boiled water in a saucer. To create the 'splash' effect, dip a new, unused toothbrush into the diluted food colour and flick the bristles with your thumb in order to splash colour all over the piece. Do not overload the toothbrush otherwise it won't colour the piece evenly. When applying the colour, position the toothbrush a few centimetres away from the object and push the bristles backwards using your thumb. This technique will give your piece more texture and you can achieve different effects by altering the consistency of the food colour. A more watery colour will result in larger, heavier droplets; a thicker consistency will create finer droplets.

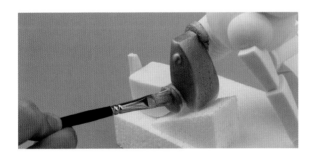

Metallic colours

Tip some metallic food colour into a saucer. Add a few drops of clear alcohol to make the consistency you need for painting and brush evenly over the piece of work. To achieve an even finish you may need to apply more than one layer of metallic paint, allowing each layer to dry fully before applying the next one. The alcohol will evaporate quickly so keep adding it as needed.

Dusting

Dip a dry, soft, round paintbrush into the dust food colour and rub the bristles on a piece of kitchen towel to remove any excess dust. Removing this excess colour will give you more control when you apply the dust to the sugar surface. I also find it useful to mix the dust with a little cornflour to ensure that the colour covers the sugar surface evenly. I use this technique when dusting figures' cheeks with Pastel Pink dust food colour.

TRANSPORTING SUGAR FIGURINES

Once you have made your sugar models you need to make sure you transport them safely to the venue where the cake will be served. These hints should help you avoid damaging your work in transit, especially if you are travelling long distances.

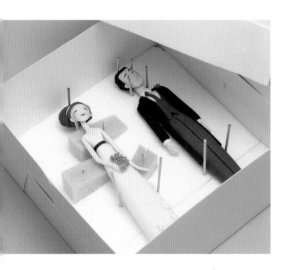

• Place the figurine, which must be fully dry, in a cake box which has a piece of polystyrene in the bottom. Stick several cocktail sticks into the polystyrene around the figurine to stop it rolling around.

• Depending on the type of figure you are transporting you can also fill in the spaces between the polystyrene base and the figure itself with soft material such as pieces of polystyrene or foam pad. This should reduce the risk of breakages, especially of more fragile pieces such as necks and arms. Look at the shape and dimensions of the figurine to see how you can support the whole structure.

• When transporting a slender figurine, place it lying down on the polystyrene as shown in the picture to prevent it from wobbling about on the cake.

• Once you have arrived at your destination, secure the figurine to the cake, pastillage base or dummy cake support with a dot of ready-made royal icing. If the figurine is slim and tall do not remove the skewer that supports the whole structure. Make sure that the recipient is aware of any skewers, dried spaghetti or other inedible items you have used to support your figures so that they can be removed safely before the cake is served.

• It is also advisable to use a dummy cake to support slender figures rather than a real cake so that the skewer remains stable throughout the whole event. Before serving the cake, the dummy cake and the figurine should be removed as one piece.

• Always make spares of any pieces that you think are likely to get damaged, such as little flowers or other small, fragile objects, and take them with you. I usually take spare pieces of paste just in case I have to fix something to the piece upon arrival.

• All these hints apply to sugar characters that are slender and more likely to break during transportation. If you don't have to take the cake anywhere or if you are making more robust figurines you may not have to take any precautions, simply place them onto the cake when they are finished.

The elegant posture of this beautiful dancer, with graceful arms and long legs, captures that special moment just before her big performance.

BALLERINA

EDIBLES

20.5cm (8") round x 7cm (2¾") deep cake, filled and crumb-coated (see pages 32 to 34)

Sugarpaste/rolled fondant: 1kg (2lb 3¼oz) pink, 150g (5¼oz) white

SK Mexican Modelling Paste (MMP): 200g (7oz) Soft Beige, 50g (1¾oz) Teddy Bear Brown

SK Sugar Florist Paste (SFP)/gum paste: 100g (3½oz) White

SK Professional Paste Food Colour: Edelweiss (white)

SK Designer Pastel Dust Food Colour: Pale Peach

SK Professional Liquid Food Colours: Chestnut, Fuchsia

50g (1¾oz) SK Instant Mix Royal Icing

EQUIPMENT

Basic equipment (see page 6)

28cm (11") round cake drum/board

20cm (8") round cake card

6cm (2³/₈") round x 6cm (2³/₈") deep polystyrene dummy

SK Great Impressions Ballerina Head Mould by Carlos Lischetti, or a mould cast from your chosen head (see page 44)

Design wheeler tool

Food-grade soft foam pad

15mm and 25mm (⁵/₈" and 1") width ribbon: white

CAKE BOARD

1   Roll out 150g (5¼oz) of white sugarpaste to a thickness of 3mm (¹/₈") and cover the cake drum. Rub a cake smoother over the paste to achieve a smooth surface then trim the excess paste from the edges with a plain-bladed knife.

2   Using a design wheeler tool and a ruler as a guide, mark lines to create a pattern as shown. Trim the excess paste from the edge if required, then glue a length of white ribbon onto the edge of the board with a non-toxic glue stick to finish. Set aside to dry.

CAKE AND DUMMY

3   Place the cake onto a cake card of the same size, then cover the cake with pink sugarpaste (see page 34). Centre the cake (complete with cake card) on the board and stick it down with a dab of royal icing. Trim the cake with a white ribbon.

4   Brush the round polystyrene dummy with edible glue and set aside. Roll out 150g (5¼oz) of pink sugarpaste on a work surface dusted with icing sugar and cover the dummy as if you were covering a round-edged cake (see page 34). Trim with white ribbon.

5   Place some royal icing into a paper piping bag (see page 8) and snip off the tip. Pipe small dots of white royal icing on the cake board at

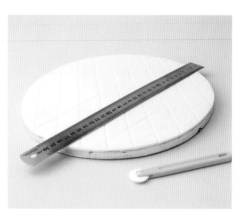

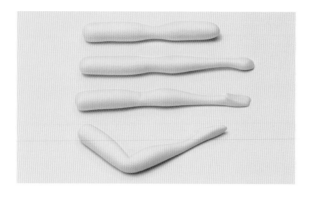

the point where the embossed lines cross, then pipe dots on the small dummy cake. Allow to dry.

TUTOR TIP

Before you start modelling the ballerina, take into account that the body proportions will depend on the size of the head mould you are using. Make a rough head with the mould you have and use this head size to guide you when making the body and limbs. Advice on basic proportions can be found on pages 42 to 43.

LEGS

6 Roll a piece of Soft Beige MMP into a sausage and stroke the paste halfway along to create the back of the knee. Roll one end into a long bottle-neck shape to create the calf, leaving a tiny piece of paste at the end. Hold this tiny piece with your thumb and index finger and use your finger to push the paste upwards slightly towards the calf to create the heel. Flatten down the remaining paste in the opposite direction to point the foot then trim the end at an angle. Make a second leg in the same way. To bend the legs, press the back of a knife into the back of the knee and bend the paste to the angle required. Bend the right leg to a right angle and the left slightly less.

7 Leave both legs to dry on a soft foam pad until the paste is firm enough to handle. Leave them to dry with the inner side of the leg facing down so that the flat side is hidden when the ballerina is assembled.

SHOES

8 Thinly roll out a small piece of White SFP on a non-stick board greased with a little vegetable fat. Cut out two teardrop (or round) shapes using a cutter and cut a 'v' shape into the rounded end. Brush the paste with a little edible glue and place it on the foot as shown in the picture. Bring the paste down and press gently to fit the shape of the foot. Trim away the excess paste with a small pair of scissors. Repeat on the other foot.

9 To make the ballet shoe ribbons, cut out a strip of White SFP and glue it to the right leg. Cut another

strip of White SFP, attach one end to the shoe on the left leg and leave it to dry in a wavy shape. You can attach the ribbons now or once you have placed the ballerina on the cake.

TUTOR TIP

Make sure you leave both legs to dry on a foam pad with the inner side facing down to prevent them from going flat.

10 Roll a small piece of White SFP into a sausage. Glue this to the legs and then onto the dummy to create the ballerina's hips.

TUTU

11 Thinly roll out some White SFP on a non-stick board and cut out five circles with a 6cm (2³/₈") round cutter. Keep the paste circles sealed in a food grade polythene bag to prevent them from drying out. Take one circle at a time and press and roll a veining tool around the edge to frill it. Glue each frilled circle to the hips with a little edible glue, layering one on top of the other. Insert a cocktail stick into the tutu, hips and dummy to support the torso later on.

TORSO AND NECK

12 Roll a small piece of White SFP into a ball. Stroke the ball at one end to make a long pear shape and create the waist. To create the décolletage, cut some paste from the wider end using a 3cm (1¹/₈") round cutter, then trim the thinner end straight using a sharp knife.

13 For the neck, roll a piece of Soft Beige MMP into a bottle shape and flatten down the wider end. Use the same round cutter as before

TUTOR TIP

It is important to have enough of the cocktail stick sticking out of the hips to support the figurine fully. The spaghetti should go all the way up through the torso once it is inserted. This will prevent the torso from bending forward whilst it dries and will support the ballerina during transportation.

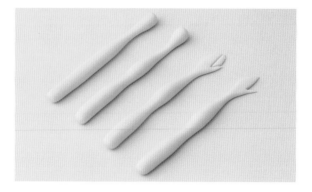

to cut the paste so that it matches the torso shape. Glue the neck to the torso and insert a cocktail stick into both the neck and torso. Leave the whole piece to firm up. Push the torso down the cocktail stick in the hips and leave to dry completely at this stage.

ARMS

14 Roll some Soft Beige MMP into a sausage and divide it in half. Stroke the paste at one end to make a wrist, leaving a tiny piece of paste at the end for the hand. Flatten the end and cut a 'v' shape into it to bring out the thumb. Trim the remaining portion into an angle to give shape to the hand. Repeat to make the other arm, making sure the thumb is on the other side.

15 Make a mark halfway along the arm with the back of a knife and bend to bring the elbow out (this

only applies to bent arms; do not make a mark if the arm is straight). Glue the arms to the torso and the left leg in the required position with a little edible glue.

TUTOR TIP

If you would like to give your ballerina fingers, make three indentations on the hand using a cutting tool.

HEAD

16 Make the head from Soft Beige MMP using the ballerina head mould or your own mould, following the instructions on page 45. Insert a cocktail stick into the neck and allow to dry.

17 Once the head has firmed up, brush the cheeks with

Pale Peach dust food colour. Paint the eyelashes and eyebrows using a fine paintbrush (no. 00) and Chestnut liquid food colour, or any brown paste food colour diluted with water to a watercolour consistency. To create a soft shadow for the eyelids, paint with Chestnut liquid food colour diluted with water. Blot any excess colour gently on a piece of kitchen paper before painting the face.

18 To paint the lips, mix Fuchsia liquid food colour with Edelweiss paste food colour to achieve a pale pink, runny consistency. Paint the lips using a fine paintbrush. Leave the head to dry completely.

TUTOR TIP

You can use fine Black or Brown and Pink food colour pens if you are not confident with using a brush.

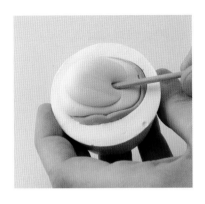

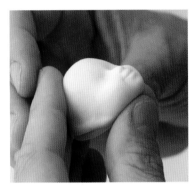

Hair

19 Roll some Teddy Bear Brown MMP into a ball, flatten slightly and glue from the back to the front of the head with a little edible glue. Bring the MMP to the forehead line and down to the back of the ears using the palm of your hand. Holding the cocktail stick, mark a few lines on the paste using the back of a modelling tool to give texture. Remove the cocktail stick and push the head down onto the cocktail stick protruding from the neck. Position the head so it is slightly tilted to one side.

20 To make the white ruffle in the hair, thinly roll out a tiny piece of White SFP and cut out a 1cm (³⁄₈") circle. Frill the edges with a cocktail stick and glue onto the top of the head. For the bun, roll a small piece of Teddy Bear Brown MMP into a sausage and roll it up. Glue to the ruffle with a little edible glue.

Assembly

21 Glue the dummy complete with ballerina onto the cake with a dab of royal icing. Ensure you remove the dummy before serving the cake: the recipient can keep it as a souvenir of the occasion.

Ballerina cake pops

Crushed digestive biscuits mixed with hazelnut paste (Nutella) or *dulce de leche* will make tasty cake pops to accompany this ballerina project. Coat them with pink-coloured tempered white chocolate and decorate each cake pop with threads of the same chocolate piped over the top. Finish each pop with a ruffle of White SFP as described in the main project: prepare them in advance and stick one to the bottom of each pop with a dot of royal icing.

Babies are always a popular subject for special cakes as they represent so many reasons to celebrate! I came up with my own formula for the proportions of a baby figure and have been modelling based on the same design for several years. You can make a baby girl using the same technique, simply by changing colours and details.

BOUNCING BABY

Edibles

15cm (6") round x 7cm (2¾") deep cake, filled and crumb-coated (see pages 32 to 34)

Sugarpaste/rolled fondant: 750g (1lb 10½oz) pale blue or white paste coloured with a touch of SK Gentian Paste Food Colour

SK Sugar Florist Paste (SFP)/gum paste: 30g (1oz) White

SK Mexican Modelling Paste (MMP): 5g (¼oz) Black, 300g (10½oz) Soft Beige, 50g (1¾oz) Teddy Bear Brown, 220g (8oz) White, 50g (1¾oz) White coloured with SK Sunny Lime Paste Food Colour

SK Professional Paste Food Colours: Berberis, Edelweiss (white), Gentian, Sunny Lime

SK Designer Pastel Dust Food Colour: Pale Peach

SK Professional Liquid Food Colour: Chestnut

Equipment

Basic equipment (see page 6)

23cm (9") round cake drum/board

15cm (6") round cake card

Hard-bristled brush, new (for texturing the paste)

15mm (⅝") width ribbon: pale blue

Cake board

1 Roll out 200g (7oz) of pale blue sugarpaste to a thickness of 5mm (just over ⅛") and cover the cake drum. Rub a cake smoother over the paste to achieve a smooth surface then trim the excess paste from the edges with a plain-bladed knife.

2 Glue the pale blue ribbon onto the side of the board with a non-toxic glue stick to give a neat finish. Texture the board by pressing a hard-bristled brush all over the surface of the sugarpaste and set aside to dry.

Body

3 To make the baby's body, roll 80g–100g (2¾oz–3½oz) of Soft Beige MMP into a pear shape. Place the body on a piece of polystyrene, then insert a skewer down the neck, all the way down through the body and into the polystyrene base. You must secure the body to the piece of polystyrene in order to support the head properly once it is placed on the body. It will also help you build the rest of the model. Set to one side.

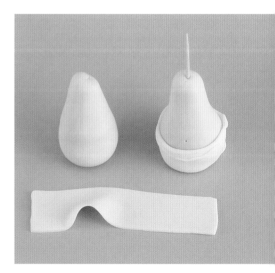

4 To make the nappy, thinly roll out a small amount of White SFP on a non-stick board greased with white vegetable fat. Cut off a strip and fold along one side to make a pleat, then glue this around the bottom of the body with a little edible glue. Trim the excess paste at the back with a pair of scissors and arrange the paste on the body. Create a few pleats by pressing

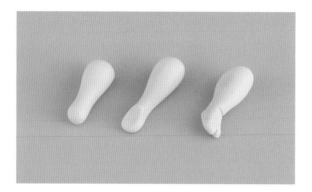

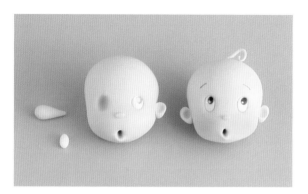

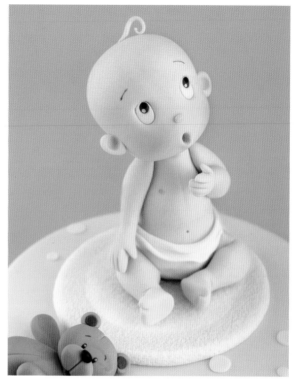

the back of a paintbrush into the paste. Make a tummy button with the tip of a cocktail stick, then paint the nipples with Chestnut liquid food colour diluted with a few drops of cooled, boiled water. Set aside to firm.

LEGS

5 Roll 30g (10oz) of Soft Beige MMP into a sausage and divide it in half. Roll each piece into a long pear shape and press down the narrower end with your fingertip to create the back of the foot and to bring out the heel. Cut a 'v' shape into the rounded end of the foot to create the big toe, then make three marks on the remaining portion to indent the rest of the toes.

6 Leave one of the legs in a straight position and bend the other one by stroking the paste at the back of

the knee and bending it to the angle required. Glue the legs onto the bottom of the body with a little edible glue. Make a few folds of skin by pressing the back of a paintbrush into the paste where the legs join the nappy.

HEAD

7 For the head, roll 100g (3½oz) of Soft Beige paste into a ball (see tip). Gently press down the middle of the ball with the side of your hand and roll the ball backwards and forwards to indent the paste and define the cheeks and forehead. If the ball gets too long and narrow, squash it from the top and bottom to keep the rounded shape required.

8 Once you are happy with the shape of the head, push it down the skewer onto the neck and position it slightly tilted to one side. Make the

rest of the facial details while the head is skewered onto the body: this way you avoid flattening the back of the head on the work surface.

9 Open up the mouth by pressing a small ball tool onto the lower half of the face, close to the bottom edge.

10 To make the nose, roll a tiny piece of Soft Beige MMP into an oval and glue it above the mouth with a little edible glue.

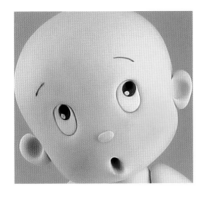

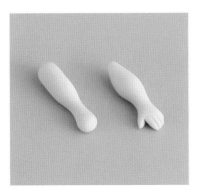

11 Make the eye sockets by gently pressing a small ball tool into the paste along the middle line along the face. Move the ball tool up and down to achieve an oval shape when making the eye sockets. When pressing the ball tool on the face, use your palm to support the back of the head.

TUTOR TIP

It is important to place the eyes on or below the imaginary middle line to make the face look like a baby (see page 43).

12 To make the eyeballs, roll two small pieces of White MMP into oval shapes and glue them into the eye sockets. Try not to overfill the sockets with paste. Push a small ball tool or the handle of a paintbrush into one corner of the eyeball where the irises will be placed.

13 For the irises, roll two tiny pieces of Teddy Bear Brown MMP (or any other colour as required) into balls and glue them to the eyeballs with a little edible glue. To finish the eyes, draw a small pupil on the iris using a Black food colour pen. Paint a white dot with White paste food colour using a fine paintbrush to give the eyes expression.

14 Use Chestnut liquid food colour and a fine paintbrush to paint the eyebrows above each eye. Dust the cheeks lightly with Pale Peach dust food colour.

15 For the ears, open a hole on each side of the head with the back of a paintbrush, following the eye line. Roll two small pieces of Soft Beige MMP into teardrop shapes and glue them to each hole with a little edible glue. Press a small ball tool into the ears to shape them.

16 To make the curl, roll a tiny piece of paste into a sausage with pointed ends and glue it onto the top of the head. Set aside to dry completely.

ARMS

17 Roll 20g–30g (¾oz–1oz) of Soft Beige MMP into a sausage and divide it in half. Stroke the sausage near the rounded end to make the wrist, leaving a tiny piece of paste to create the hand. Flatten down the piece of paste slightly and make a 'v' shape cut on one side of the rounded end to bring out the thumb. Make three marks

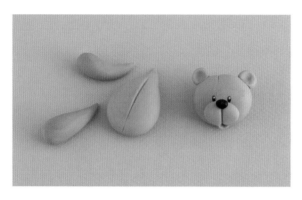
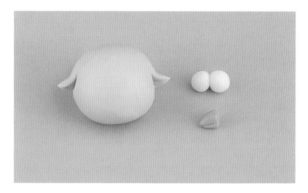

on the remaining portion to indent fingers. To bring the index finger out, make a tiny cut with scissors in order to separate it from the rest of the fingers. Push the other three fingers slightly down to shape the hand, leaving the index finger pointing out.

18 Glue the arms to the side of the body as shown in the picture, trimming any excess paste from the wider end if required, and set aside.

TEDDY BEAR

19 Roll 30g (1oz) of Teddy Bear Brown paste into a sausage and split it in half. Roll one piece into a ball and flatten it down for the head. Roll the other piece into a teardrop shape for the body, flatten it slightly and mark halfway along with a cutting modelling tool. Set to one side.

20 To make the snout of the bear, roll a tiny piece of paste into an oval shape and glue it onto the lower half of the head. Press the back of a knife into the snout to divide it in two, then open up the mouth on the lower half of the snout with the tip of a cocktail stick.

21 To make the nose, roll a tiny piece of Black MMP into an oval shape and glue it onto the upper part of the snout. Draw two tiny dots for the eyes, just above the snout, using a Black food colour pen. Blush the cheeks with Pale Peach dust colour using a dry paintbrush. For the ears, roll two balls of paste and glue them onto the head with a little edible glue. Press into each one with a small ball tool.

22 To make the arms and legs, roll 20g (¾oz) of Teddy Bear Brown MMP into a sausage and divide

it into four pieces. Roll each piece of paste into a teardrop and set aside.

23 Once all the pieces are made, glue them together with a little edible glue straight onto the cake in the required position.

STUFFED BIRD

24 Roll 50g (1¾oz) of Sunny Lime coloured MMP into a ball. For the wings, make a cut on each side of the ball using a pair of scissors.

25 To make the patch on the front, knead some Sunny Lime MMP with a little White MMP to achieve a pale green colour, then thinly roll out the paste and cut out a teardrop shape. Glue it to the front of the body with a little edible glue. Make the sewn join on the front by pressing the tip of a cocktail stick down the middle of the body.

26 For the beak, colour a tiny amount of white MMP with Berberis food colour. Roll this into a cone and glue it above the patch at the front. To make the eyes, roll two balls of White paste and glue them above the beak. Use a Black food colour pen to draw a small black dot in the middle of each eye.

27 To make the hair on top, roll some of the pale green paste into a thin sausage and cut it into five segments. Stick them together at one end with a little edible glue then glue them on top of the head, above the eyes. Set aside to dry.

CAKE

28 Cover the cake with the pale blue sugarpaste as described on page 34. Position the cake in the centre of the board and stick the cake in place with a dab of royal icing. Trim the cake with a pale blue ribbon around the bottom, securing in place with a dab of edible glue or royal icing.

RUG

29 To make the round rug, roll 200g (7oz) of white sugarpaste into a ball and flatten it down with a cake smoother to a circle approximately 10cm (4") in diameter. Thinly roll out some pale blue sugarpaste and cut out a circle and a ring using three different round cutters. Centre and glue the circle and the ring shape onto the white paste and press down with the brush to integrate the two colours and give texture to the rug at the same time.

FINISHING TOUCHES

30 Place the rug onto the cake so that it is slightly off-centre. Take the baby off the polystyrene base, leaving the skewer sticking out at the bottom of the body (you might need to trim the skewer before inserting it into the cake). Place the baby onto the rug and glue it in place with a dab of royal icing.

31 Place the teddy bear to one side of the rug and the stuffed bird onto the board, gluing each of them in place with dots of royal icing. Cut circles from White MMP using a round nozzle or small round cutters and glue them to the cake and board to finish the cake.

MARZIPAN BITES

To model these cute birdies out of marzipan, simply follow the instructions given in the Bouncing Baby project. These can be placed around the cake for display and make gorgeous take-home treats for children.

For a different flavour you can mix some pistachio flavouring into the marzipan; this will also colour it green without having to add any food colours.

Colours play an important role in cake decorating as they can set the tone for each piece. Red would have been an instinctive choice for this project, but Elio and I decided to go for blue hues instead to give an original, fresh look to our little queen. The heart is highlighted with a touch of red at the top of her sceptre.

QUEEN OF HEARTS

20cm (8") round x 14cm (5½") deep bowl-shaped cake, filled and crumb-coated (see pages 32 to 34)

Sugarpaste/rolled fondant: 1.3kg (2lb 13¾oz) white

SK Mexican Modelling Paste (MMP): 150g (5¼oz) Soft Beige, 50g (1¾oz) White

SK Sugar Florist Paste (SFP): 50g (1¾oz) White

SK Professional Paste Food Colours: Edelweiss (white), Hydrangea, Poppy, Teddy Bear Brown, Terracotta, Vine

SK Designer Pastel Dust Food Colour: Pale Peach

SK Metallic Lustre Dust Food Colour: Antique Gold

SK Professional Liquid Food Colours: Blackberry, Poppy, Teddy Bear Brown

150g (5¼oz) SK Instant Mix Royal Icing

SK CMC Gum

Marshmallow piped in 2 dome shapes

Equipment

Basic equipment (see page 6)

25cm (10") cake drum/board

20cm (8") cake card

Assorted heart cutters in three different sizes

Shell modelling tool

Piping nozzles: nos. 1, 2, 10

15mm (⅝") width ribbon: light blue

Templates (see page 182)

Cotton wool

Cake board

1 Colour 200g (7oz) of sugarpaste a light Hydrangea colour, roll out to a thickness of 3mm (⅛") and cover the cake board. Rub a smoother over the paste to remove any imperfections and trim the excess paste from the edges with a plain-bladed knife. Glue a length of light blue ribbon onto the edge of the board with a non-toxic glue stick and set aside to dry.

Tutor Tip

Make the following pieces in advance to allow for drying time.

Lace piece

2 Thinly roll out some White SFP on a non-stick board greased with a little white vegetable fat. Cut out the collar shape using the template provided and a sharp knife. To achieve a neat edge, leave the paste stuck to the board. Cut out the small circles of the template using a 1cm (⅜") round nozzle. Use no. 1 and 2 nozzles to emboss the SFP and create a pattern. Leave to dry with a ball of cotton wool underneath both sides to give shape, as shown.

Tutor Tip

I would recommend making two of these lace pieces from flower paste in case one of them breaks when you are handling the piece. They only take a few minutes to make and will help to avoid a headache later on!

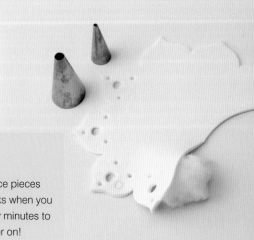

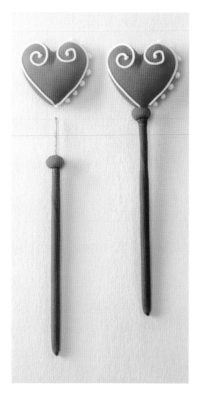

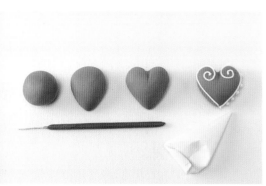

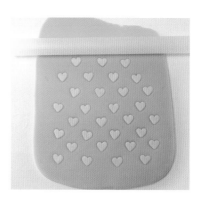

CROWN

3 Roll 20g (¾oz) of White SFP into a cone shape. Press a ball tool into the wider end to hollow it out then use the tool to thin out the edge. Cut the paste into pointed tips using a small pair of scissors. Pipe small dots of white royal icing onto each pointed end and leave to dry for a couple of minutes. Paint the crown with gold dust food colour diluted with clear alcohol. Set aside to dry.

HEART-SHAPED SCEPTRE

4 To make the sceptre cut an 11cm (4½") piece of wooden skewer. Roll a small piece of Teddy Bear Brown-coloured sugarpaste into a ball. Moisten the skewer with a little edible glue and push it through the ball, then

roll the paste so that it covers almost the whole length of the skewer. Trim off the excess paste, leaving a piece of skewer protruding from one end. Set aside to dry.

5 For the heart, roll 30g (1oz) of Poppy-coloured MMP into a teardrop shape, using the template as a size reference. Press the back of a knife down the middle of the rounded side to make a heart shape. Use a small paper piping bag to pipe lines and dots of soft-peak royal icing onto the heart then set aside to dry. When dry, paint the lines and dots with Gold metallic dust food colour diluted with a few drops of clear alcohol. Roll a tiny ball of Poppy MMP and push this onto the skewer then insert the skewer into the heart shape and secure with a little edible glue.

Important note: Always tell the recipient when inedible supports are used in a

cake that they must be removed from the cake before it is served.

CAKE

6 Stick the cake onto the covered cake board with a dab of royal icing.

7 To make the underskirt, roll some dark Vine-coloured sugarpaste to a thickness of 5mm (just over ⅛"). Grease the surface of the rolled paste with a little vegetable fat then cover it with a cling film to keep the paste moist whilst you are cutting out the little hearts.

8 Roll out some pale Vine sugarpaste on a non-stick board to a thickness of 2mm (just under ⅛") and cut out little heart shapes. Arrange the hearts on the dark Vine sugarpaste

in alternate rows, pressing gently to stick them to the paste. Roll over them gently with a rolling pin to merge the hearts with the paste. Cut the paste into a triangle shape and stick it to the front of the cake, rubbing gently with the palm of your hand to secure the paste in place.

TUTOR TIP

The sugarpaste used to cut out the hearts has to be soft enough to stick to the other paste. If it is too dry it won't stick properly.

9 For the skirt, roll some dark Hydrangea-coloured sugarpaste to a thickness of 5mm (just over $^{1}/_{8}$") and cover the rest of the cake from the back to the front. Stroke the paste gently to shape it and to smooth out

any pleats on the narrower part of the cake at the top. Trim the paste neatly with a sharp knife.

10 Knead the trimmings of the dark Hydrangea sugarpaste with a pinch of CMC gum to give the paste extra strength for modelling the torso and sleeves. Roll some dark Hydrangea paste into a ball and glue on top of the skirt with a little edible glue. Press gently onto the cake to flatten the ball slightly.

11 For the collar, roll some Vine-coloured MMP to 3mm ($^{1}/_{8}$") and cut out a 3cm (1$^{1}/_{8}$") circle. Glue the circle to the top of the torso with a little edible glue. Emboss concentric circles onto the paste using different sized round cutters. Roll a thin sausage of pale Vine paste and glue it around the collar to finish.

12 For the edge of the skirt, roll some white sugarpaste into two thick, tapered sausages. Starting at the narrower end, glue them from the bottom of the torso down the skirt (covering the join of the inner skirt and dress) and around the bottom of the cake and the board. Make sure they meet at the back then trim neatly at the join. To achieve the fur effect, use a paintbrush to brush the edge of the skirt with white soft-peak royal icing. Evenly brush the royal icing across a small portion of the trim, then stipple the icing using a flat brush with hard bristles to create a fur texture.

13 Roll tiny pieces of Hydrangea sugarpaste into balls. Press and glue them to the fur with a little edible glue. To make the frill at the front, roll some pale Vine MMP into a sausage and glue to the front with a little edible glue. Press with a shell modelling tool to give texture, as shown.

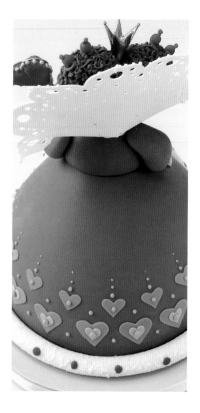

14 To make the heart pattern around the skirt you will need small, medium and large heart cutters and two lighter shades of Hydrangea paste (mix the sugarpaste trimmings with White MMP). Thinly roll out the light Hydrangea paste, cut out several large heart shapes and glue them around the bottom of the dress so they sit in a row. Make a second row of medium hearts and glue them above and in between the bigger ones below.

15 Cut out smaller hearts of the lightest Hydrangea colour and glue them onto the larger hearts. Pipe dots of Hydrangea-coloured royal icing to complete the heart design as shown.

ARMS

16 Roll a ball of dark Hydrangea sugarpaste into a sausage and divide it in two. Roll each sausage into a thick cone shape. Open up the sleeve at the wider end with a medium ball tool. Glue the sleeves to the torso in the required position with a little edible glue.

17 Roll some Soft Beige MMP into a sausage and divide it in half for the hands. Stroke each sausage at one end to create the wrist, leaving a tiny piece of paste at the end for the hand. Flatten the hand and cut out a 'v' shape with a small pair of scissors to bring out the thumb. Indent the fingers on the remaining portion with a cutting tool. To give the queen more attitude, make a cut at the indentation of the little finger and curve it slightly as shown. Leave the hands to firm up. Once

firm, glue into the sleeves with a little softened paste in the required position.

HEAD

18 Roll some Soft Beige MMP into a rounded pear shape. To make the eyes, use a fine Black food colour pen or a fine paintbrush and Blackberry liquid food colour to paint two dots. The eyes fall on the middle line of the face. Make two tiny dots of white paste food colour and stick them to the edge of the eyes to highlight them.

TUTOR TIP

If you prefer, you can take some Edelweiss paste food colour on the tip of a cocktail stick and touch gently on the surface to create a tiny dot on each eye.

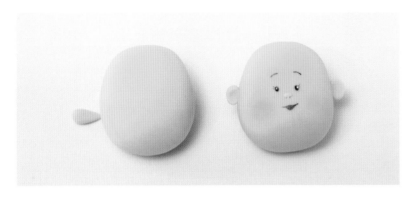

19 For the nose roll a tiny piece of Soft Beige MMP into an oval shape and glue below and in between the eyes. Press with the pointed end of a cocktail stick to open up the nostrils. Paint tiny lips with Poppy liquid food colour and a fine paintbrush. Use a soft round paintbrush to dust the cheeks with Pale Peach dust food colour.

20 For the ears, make a hole on each side of the head, following the eye line. Roll two tiny pieces of Soft Beige paste into teardrops and stick them into the holes with a little edible glue. Press a small ball tool into each ear to give shape. Using Teddy Bear Brown liquid food colour and a fine paintbrush, paint thin lines above the eyes for the eyebrows. Leave the head to firm up for a while.

HAIR

21 As the queen's hair is quite large, I have used marshmallow domes to give it volume. Marshmallow is light and gives volume without adding extra weight to the piece so it is useful for this type of work. Glue two pieces of marshmallow onto the head with a dot of stiff royal icing and leave to dry. Skewer the head onto the torso.

22 To make the hair, colour 50g (1¾oz) of royal icing with Terracotta paste food colour. Fill a small paper piping bag and snip off the very end, or fit the piping bag with a no. 2 round nozzle to create the curls. Pipe curly hair all over the marshmallow, over the back and sides of the head and up to the forehead line. When piping, apply more pressure to the back to create a

curly texture. Try to give the hairstyle a heart shape whilst you are piping. Place the little crown in the middle before the royal icing dries completely.

FINISHING TOUCHES

23 Glue the sceptre to the left hand in the position required with a dot of softened sugarpaste or MMP. Glue the lace piece to the back of the head with a dab of stiff white royal icing (the lace piece should stick easily to the hair as it is not heavy). If required, support the lace piece with a few skewers whilst it dries. To finish, decorate the hair with tiny balls of Terracotta and Poppy MMP as shown in the main picture.

HEART BISCUITS

For an afternoon tea fit for a queen, bake heart-shaped biscuits for your guests. Outline the biscuits with soft-peak white royal icing using a paper piping bag and a no. 2 round nozzle. Let the icing dry for a few minutes.

Fill in the biscuits with run-out royal icing tinted with any of the colours used for the main project. For the dotted hearts, pipe dots of run-out white royal icing while the surface of the first coating is still wet and let the colours blend into one pattern.

For the red or white hearts, let the run-out icing form a crust. Use a small paper piping bag fitted with a no. 1 nozzle to pipe white medium-consistency royal icing into heart-shaped scrolls. Pipe small dots of icing on the outline to create the lace effect. Let the biscuits dry completely before wrapping in cellophane or storing in a presentation box.

I grew up surrounded by movies where robots and creatures from outer space were always the stars of the show. Those movies inspired me to make my own menacing, defiant and almost human-looking robot. I used the original concept design as a basic reference but changed the shapes of the body parts as I created the sugar model. The 'threading' technique I developed to build up the character can be used to create your own interesting, animated models.

ROBOT

EDIBLES

15cm (6") round sponge cake, slightly chamfered, filled and crumb-coated (see pages 32 to 34)

Sugarpaste/rolled fondant: 700g (1lb 8¾oz) white

SK Instant Mix Pastillage: 1kg (2lb ¾oz)

SK Mexican Modelling Paste (MMP): small amount of Black, 110g (4oz) White

SK Designer Metallic Lustre Dust Food Colour: Silver

SK Professional Liquid Food Colours: Gentian, Hydrangea, Lilac

SK Instant Mix Royal Icing: 100g (3½oz)

EQUIPMENT

Basic equipment (see page 6)

25cm (10") round cake drum/board

2 x 15cm (6") round cake cards

20cm (8") cake card

Spacers: 3cm (1¹⁄₈"), 1cm (³⁄₈"), 5mm (just over ¹⁄₈"), 3mm (¹⁄₈") (You can stack three 1cm levellers to get the 3cm height if you are unable to get these in the shops)

6cm (2³⁄₈") polystyrene sphere

22-gauge floral wire: white

Thin metal skewer

Thin piece of cardboard

15mm (⁵⁄₈") width ribbon: black

Templates (see pages 182 to 183)

CAKE BOARD

1 Roll out 150g (5¼oz) of white sugarpaste to a thickness of 3mm (¹⁄₈") and cover the cake drum. Rub a cake smoother over the paste to achieve a smooth surface. Trim the excess paste from the edges with a plain-bladed knife. Glue a black ribbon to the edge of the board with a non-toxic glue stick and set aside to dry.

2 Place the cake onto a cake card of the same size. Cover the cake with white sugarpaste (see page 34) and brush with a layer of Silver metallic dust food colour diluted with a few drops of clear alcohol. Stick the cake (complete with cake card) centrally onto the board with a dab of royal icing. Finish the cake with a length of black ribbon. Dowel the cake to prevent the cake-top decoration from sinking into it (see page 38).

PASTILLAGE BASE

3 Roll out some white pastillage to a thickness of 5mm (just over ¹⁄₈") and cut out two 20cm (8") circles using a cake tin or cake card as a guide. Use a sharp knife to get a clean, neat cut. Emboss the inner circle by pressing a 16cm (6½") round tin into the paste whilst it is still soft. Leave to dry. Roll out more white pastillage to a thickness of 1cm (³⁄₈") and cut out a 10cm (4") circle using a tin or paper template as a guide. Leave to dry. Thinly roll out some Black MMP and cut out two curved strips. Stick these to the pastillage base with edible glue to add movement.

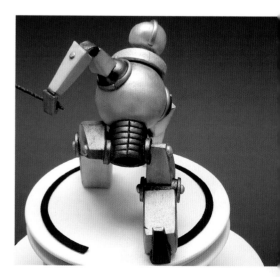

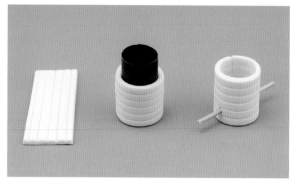

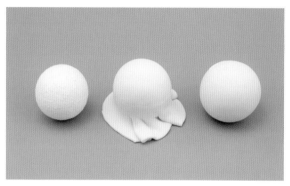

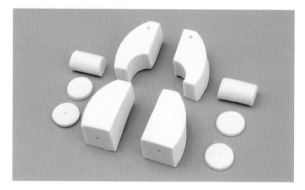

Assembly

4 Stick the 10cm (4") pastillage base to the centre of the 20cm (8") base with royal icing. Roll some Hydrangea sugarpaste into a sausage shape and glue this around the 10cm (4") pastillage disc with a little edible glue. Stick the other 20cm (8") piece of pastillage on top of the other two with royal icing and leave to dry.

ROBOT

Torso

5 Cover the polystyrene sphere with royal icing. This will work as glue for the pastillage to stick to firmly. Roll some white pastillage to a thickness of 3mm (¹/₈") and cover the sphere. Bring the paste down to the bottom and trim the excess paste with a plain-bladed knife. Smooth the surface by rolling the sphere between your hands and then leave to dry.

Hips

6 Roll out some white pastillage to a thickness of 5mm (just over ¹/₈") and cut out a rectangle using the template provided. Mark lines lengthways along the rectangle and wrap it around a card cylinder 3cm (1¹/₈") in diameter.

Leave the paste to firm for 30 minutes and then remove the former.

7 While the paste is still soft, push a wooden skewer into the bottom end to create a hole. This will be where the legs are inserted later on. Leave the skewer inserted until the piece is fully dry, then remove. Once the torso and hips are fully dry, glue them together with royal icing and leave to dry again.

Legs

8 Roll out some white pastillage to a thickness of 3cm (1¹/₈") and cut out the upper and lower parts of the legs respectively, using the templates provided. To achieve a neat cut, use a knife for the straight edges of the template and round cutters for the curved ones. Pierce the top end of the upper part of the leg with a wooden

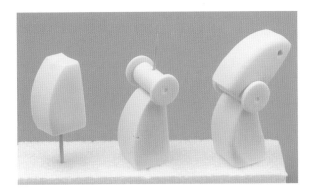

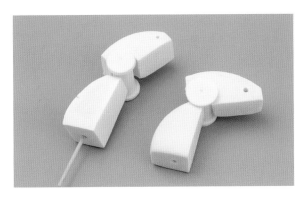

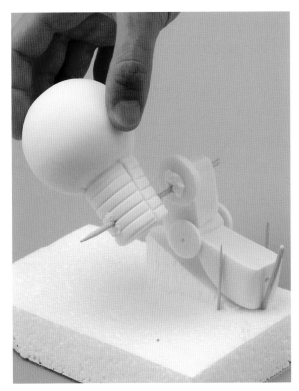

skewer to create a hole into which the hips will be threaded later on. For the knee, roll some pastillage into a sausage 2cm (¾") thick x 3cm (1⅛") long.

9 Roll some more white pastillage to 3mm (⅛") and cut out four 2.5cm (1") circles using a round cutter. Press the handle of a paintbrush down into the centre of each circle while the paste is still soft. Leave all the pieces to firm up.

Left leg assembly

10 Insert a wooden skewer halfway up from the bottom of the lower part of the leg and push it into a polystyrene base so that it is easier to handle. Glue the knee to the lower part with softened pastillage and push a cocktail stick through it, leaving part of it sticking out. Glue the circles to the sides of the knee with softened pastillage. Push the upper leg into the cocktail stick and glue it at an angle of approximately 45°. Use pieces of polystyrene as support for the leg and leave to dry.

Right leg assembly

11 Follow the same procedure as for the left leg but this time, glue the upper part of the right leg at an angle of approximately 90°.

Attaching the torso to the legs

12 Place the right leg on a piece of polystyrene as shown and secure with cocktail sticks to prevent the leg from falling sideways or backwards. Cut two circles of pastillage and glue them onto the inner side of each leg while they are still fresh. Push a wooden skewer through the right leg and hips and secure the pieces in place with softened pastillage in a piping bag (see page 8). The fresh circles of pastillage will act as a cushion and help the legs stick to the hips. Finally, pierce the skewer through the left leg and stick it in place with softened pastillage.

13 Let the torso lean forward onto the left leg, which should support its weight. When the structure is completely dry, use pliers to trim any extra bits of the skewer which may be sticking out from either side. Cover them with a piece of pastillage rolled into a ball and attach with edible glue.

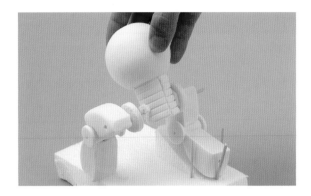
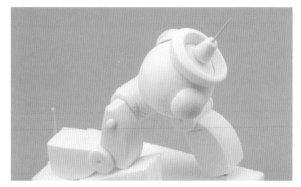
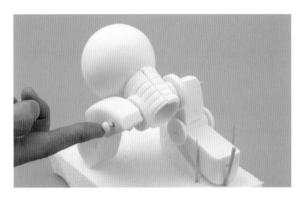
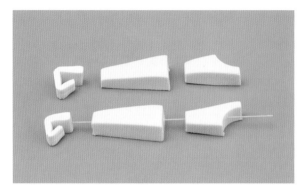

Shoulders

14 Roll some pastillage into two 3cm (1¹/₈") hemispheres and let them firm up. Glue them to the side of the torso with a little softened pastillage.

Collar

15 Roll out some pastillage to a thickness of 1.5cm (⁵/₈") and cut out a ring using 5cm (2") and 3.5cm (1³/₈") round cutters. Pinch one side slightly to give a teardrop shape and glue to the torso with a little edible glue while the pastillage is still fresh.

Neck

16 Roll some pastillage into a cone shape and trim the ends. Heat up a thin metal skewer and insert it into the torso, creating a hole. Insert a cocktail stick through the neck and into the hole in the torso, securing with softened pastillage. Leave to dry.

Arms and hands

17 Roll out the pastillage to a thickness of 1.5cm (⁵/₈") for the arms and cut out each part using the templates. For the hands, roll out the pastillage to a thickness of 3mm (¹/₈") and cut out the trapezoid shape using the template. Mark a line along one side and indent two marks on the opposite side with the back of a knife. Bend as shown in the picture.

18 Once all the pieces are firm enough to handle (but not completely dry), push a piece of wire down through the centre of each part and start threading them together. This wire is only temporary at this stage to create the holes for the final assembly. Do not glue the pieces together at this stage.

Right arm assembly

19 Insert a piece of wire down through the right shoulder (which should still be soft inside; if not pierce a hole with a hot metal skewer). Thread the wire through the arm and glue it to the shoulder, then thread the forearm onto the wire and glue it to the arm.

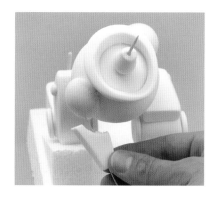
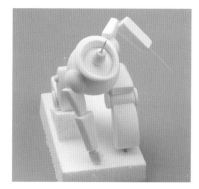
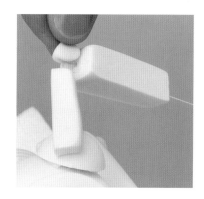
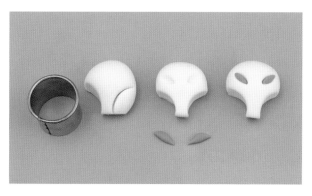
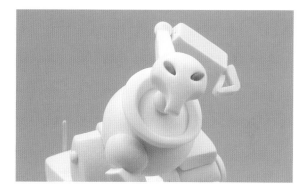

Left arm assembly

20 Insert a piece of wire into
the left shoulder. Thread
the arm onto the wire and glue with a
little softened pastillage. Leave to dry
completely before adding and gluing
the forearm.

21 Bend the wire at the elbow,
then thread the forearm onto
the wire. Glue the two pieces together
with a small piece of fresh pastillage.
Wait until the arm and forearm are
completely dry before threading and
gluing the hand.

Head

22 Roll some pastillage into a ball
approximately 4cm (1½") in
diameter and flatten it down slightly. Press
a 3cm (1⅛") round cutter into the sides
of the lower half to make the head shape
as shown. Press a Dresden tool into the
upper half to create the eye sockets. Roll
two tiny pieces of Gentian coloured MMP
into a teardrop shape and glue them into
the eye sockets with a little edible glue.
Leave the head to firm up.

23 Push the head onto the cocktail
stick in the neck and place in

TUTOR TIP

Using wire to pierce through the parts of the figure (which I call the 'threading
technique'), makes it easy to hold the different parts firmly in place. It helps to
manoeuvre the figure into a certain posture as you can bend the wire to the
required position.

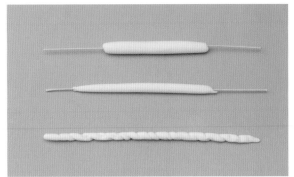

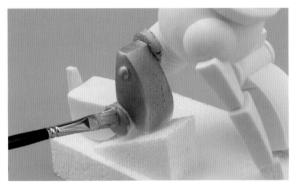

the required position to give your robot a menacing look. Glue a thin strip of pastillage down the forehead as a finishing touch.

Feet

24 Roll out some pastillage into a wedge, making the thicker side approximately 1.5cm (⅝") deep. Place the template onto the wedge with the heel facing the thinner end and cut out the feet.

SPEAR

25 Cut a 12cm (5") piece of floral wire. Roll a small piece of pastillage into a ball. Moisten the wire with a little edible glue and push it through the ball. Roll the pastillage again in order to cover the whole length of the wire. Trim any excess paste from the ends and make a few marks along the sides with a cocktail stick. Glue to the left hand once completely dry.

PAINTING

26 Paint the surface of the robot with Silver metallic dust food colour diluted with a few drops of clear alcohol. Apply a second coat of Lilac liquid food colour to darken the joints, hips, spear and feet.

ASSEMBLY

27 Glue the feet of the robot to the pastillage base with a dot of softened pastillage. Leave to dry completely.

28 For transportation, place the robot on the base in a separate box with a piece of polystyrene at the bottom. Stick several skewers into the polystyrene around the figurine to stop it from moving. Once the cake has been placed on the presentation table, stick the pastillage base and robot onto the cake with a dot of royal icing.

Robot heads

Bake hemispheres 6cm (2³/₈") in diameter using any of the sponge cake recipes given on pages 9 to 14. Once the mini cakes have cooled, cut out two small hemispheres on one side of the cake using a 2cm (¾") round cutter to give a sort of 'skull' shape to the head. Seal the crumb with a layer of chocolate ganache or buttercream and chill in the fridge for a couple of hours before coating.

Stick the mini cakes onto round cake cards that are slightly bigger than the heads. Cover the cakes and bases all in one with white sugarpaste, pressing the paste gently to give shape. Trim the excess paste from around the edges using a round cutter the same size as the cake base to create a neat edge. Press the blunt side of a round cutter into the paste to give texture and highlight the robot's jaw line. Glue a strip of paste onto the head up to the eye line.

Press the top of a Dresden tool into the paste to create the eye sockets. Paint the whole piece with Silver dust food colour diluted with clear alcohol. Highlight some areas with Lilac liquid food colour. Fill the eye sockets with Gentian sugarpaste modelled into sausages with pointed ends.

You can also give the heads a rougher look by making marks randomly with a knife or by pressing the hard bristles of a brush into the paste while it is still fresh.

When I decided to include a fairy in a cake design, my brother Elio came up with one of his beautiful drawings inspired by nature, hence the name Flora. Before you bake and cover the cake, model the fairy figure and flowers in advance to allow for drying time.

FLORA THE WOODLAND FAIRY

EDIBLES

12cm (5") diameter x 10cm (4") tall roulade filled with ganache (or buttercream if you prefer) (see recipe on page 12)

Marshmallow pieces (see recipe on page 23)

Sugarpaste/rolled fondant: 500g (1lb 1¾oz) white, 200g (7oz) white coloured with pale Daffodil (yellow) and a touch of Teddy Bear Brown Paste Food Colours

SK Mexican Modelling Paste (MMP): tiny amount of White, plus 250g (8¾oz) White coloured with a touch of Sunny Lime Paste Food Colour

SK Sugar Florist Paste (SFP)/gum paste: 100g (3½oz) White

SK Professional Paste Food Colours: Daffodil (yellow), Edelweiss (white), Olive, Sunny Lime, Teddy Bear Brown

SK Professional Dust Food Colours: Daffodil (yellow), Green Envy

SK Professional Liquid Food Colours: Blackberry (black), Bulrush, Chestnut, Daffodil (yellow), Holly/Ivy

100g (3½oz) SK Instant Mix Royal Icing

Small piece of rice paper (to make the wings)

EQUIPMENT

Basic equipment (see page 6)

28cm (11") round cake drum/board

2 x 15cm (6") round cake cards (one as a base for the roulade and a spare to handle the cake)

SK Great Impressions Fairy Head Mould by Carlos Lischetti, or a mould cast from your chosen head (see page 44)

Flower cutters in various shapes and sizes

Star piping nozzle

New, hard-bristled brush

Airbrush (or new toothbrush)

15mm (⅝") width ribbon: sage green

Template for wings (see page 183)

TUTOR TIP

Before you start making the fairy, remember that the proportions of the body will depend on the size of the head mould you are using. Guidelines on body proportions are given on pages 42 to 43.

HEAD

1   Use White MMP coloured with Sunny Lime to make the head from the mould (see instructions on page 45).

2   Once the head is complete and whilst the paste is still soft, press a medium ball tool onto the eye line to create big eye sockets. Give shape to the jaw line by smoothing the paste with your thumb. Open the nostrils with the tip of a cocktail stick and set the head aside to firm.

3   To make the eyes, roll two tiny pieces of White MMP into balls. Glue to the eye sockets with a little

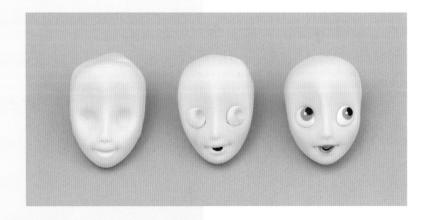

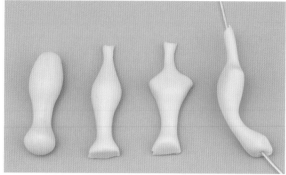

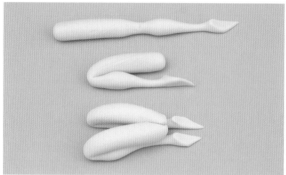

edible glue to fill in the socket. Press a small ball tool into the upper half of the white eyeball to create the socket into which the irises will be inserted (this socket can be moved depending on the direction in which you want the fairy to look).

4 To make the irises, roll tiny pieces of Olive-coloured MMP and glue to the sockets. Press gently to smooth the surface of the eyes.

5 Use a fine paintbrush to paint the pupils with Holly/Ivy liquid food colour. Note that the pupil has to touch the edge of the eyeball. When dry, paint a dot of Edelweiss paste food colour onto the iris to highlight the expression of the eyes.

6 To paint the lips, mix Holly/Ivy liquid food colour and Edelweiss paste food colour to achieve a lighter shade of green. Paint the lower and upper lips using a fine paintbrush. Paint a dark green line in between the lips with Holly/Ivy liquid food colour to give depth.

7 To make the front teeth, roll a tiny piece of White MMP into a thin sausage and glue to the inner part of the mouth. Use the tip of a modelling tool to help you place this small piece of paste. Dust the cheeks with a mixture of Green Envy and Daffodil dust food colours.

TORSO, WAIST AND HIPS

8 To make the torso, waist and hips in one piece, roll a ball of Sunny Lime-coloured MMP slightly bigger than the amount of paste used for the head. Roll this ball into a sausage then stroke the paste down $2/3$ of the length to create the waist. Roll the other end into a bottleneck shape to bring the neck out. Flatten down the sausage gently and pinch each side of the neck to bring the shoulders out. Curve the shape of the waist as shown in the picture.

9 Push a cocktail stick into the neck and chest and push another piece into the bottom end at the hips. Leave to dry on the side that will be facing towards the back of the cake in the required position.

TUTOR TIP

Make the waist thinner and longer than usual to give the fairy a delicate, slender look. The cocktail stick inserted into the torso is important as it will give structure to the body.

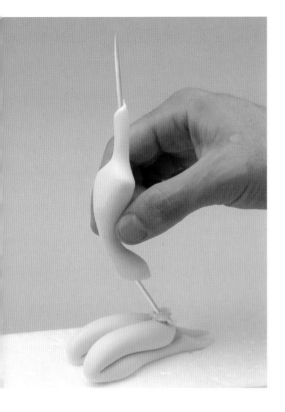

LEGS

10 Roll some Sunny Lime-coloured MMP into a sausage shape and stroke the middle of this piece to narrow the leg at the knee. Stroke one end into a long bottleneck shape to create the calf, leaving a tiny piece of paste at the end for the foot. Hold the tiny piece at the end using your thumb and index finger and push the paste upwards (in the direction of the calf) using your fingertip to create the heel. Flatten down the remaining portion in the opposite direction to give shape to the foot and trim the end to a point.

11 To bend the leg, press the back of the knee with the back of a knife and bend fully. Make a second leg in the same way, then glue them together at the thigh and set aside to dry.

ASSEMBLING THE TORSO AND LEGS

TUTOR TIP

Place the legs on a piece of polystyrene to help support the figure whilst you are working.

12 Insert the cocktail stick in the base of the torso into the thighs, pushing it through both thighs and down into the polystyrene. Glue both parts together with a little softened Sunny Lime MMP. Trim the bottom end of the torso with a sharp knife if needed so that it sits comfortably on the legs. If necessary, fill in the space between the hips and legs with a little softened paste.

13 Pipe tiny dots of white royal icing onto the bottom and hips to create the costume; this should give texture and even out the join between the hips and thighs. Set aside to dry. Once the piped icing has dried, dust with Daffodil dust food colour to blend the icing with the body.

TUTOR TIP

Piped royal icing not only gives texture but makes the whole structure solid.

ARMS

14 Roll a ball of Sunny Lime MMP into a sausage. Stroke the paste halfway to create the elbow. Stroke the forearm into a

long, bottleneck shape to make a wrist, leaving a tiny piece of paste at the end for the hand. Flatten the hand and cut a 'v' shape to bring out the thumb. Trim the remaining portion to a point to represent the fingers.

15 Mark the elbow halfway along inside of the arm with the back of a knife and bend to bring the elbow out (this only applies to bent arms, so do not make a mark if the arm is straight).

16 Glue the arms to the shoulders with a little edible glue and blend the join by rubbing the paste gently with your finger. Bend the wrists to make the hands sit comfortably on the polystyrene block, following the photograph to see how the arms are positioned in front of the body. If the arms are straight, give them a natural look by bending slightly at the elbows, otherwise they will look stiff.

TUTOR TIP

It is very important to place the right arm on the side of the leg as this will help to give stability to the whole piece and prevent the model from leaning sideways.

17 Push the head down onto the cocktail stick that is sticking out of the neck in the required position, and secure it to the back with some modelling paste. Leave to dry fully at this stage.

HAIR

18 To give volume to the hair, glue pieces of marshmallow onto the top, sides and back of the head using royal icing. To make the hair, fill a

paper piping bag with Olive-coloured royal icing and snip off the very end. Evenly pipe a layer of royal icing along the marshmallow and texture with a damp brush. Once the first layer of icing has dried, pipe scrolls of a lighter tone to add extra texture. Make the fringe by piping lines of royal icing at the front of the head.

TUTOR TIP

Using pieces of marshmallow is a useful way to give volume to the hair without adding too much weight to the head.

EARS

19 Roll a small piece of Sunny Lime MMP into a sausage and

divide it in half. Roll each piece into a sausage with pointed ends. Press a ball tool into each sausage to give shape and, following the eye line, glue to the sides of the head and the hair.

FLOWERS

20 To make the flowers, thinly roll some White SFP on a non-stick board greased with a little vegetable fat. Cut out different flowers using two or three different cutters of your choice, then press a ball tool into the SFP to smooth out the edges and give the flowers shape. Once the flowers have firmed, dust the centres with Daffodil and Green Envy dust food colours. Glue the flowers to the hair with a dot of royal icing and pipe more dots of white royal icing in the centre to finish.

SMALL BUTTERFLIES

21 Thinly roll out some White SFP on a non-stick board greased with a little vegetable fat and cut out a flower shape with pointed petals. Trim the flower to make a two-petal shape. Press a ball tool onto the SFP to soften the edges, bend in half and pinch to give a wing shape. Let them dry before painting with Blackberry liquid food colour using a fine paintbrush.

22 Glue the small butterflies and flowers to the hair with dots of royal icing.

WINGS

23 Cut the wings out of rice paper using the template provided as a guide. Fold the wings in half and glue to the fairy's back with a dot of soft royal icing. Remove the excess icing with a fine paintbrush and leave to dry.

CAKE

24 To transform the cake into a tree stump, make several cuts into the side of the cake using a serrated knife as shown. Spread a layer of ganache onto the top and down the sides of the cake to seal the crumb and

TUTOR TIP

To save time you could also use Black SFP to make the butterflies.

help attach the sugarpaste. Chill in the fridge for a couple of hours before coating.

25 Roll out some white sugarpaste to a thickness of 5mm (just over 1/8") on a work surface dusted with icing sugar. Roll the paste to a diameter slightly bigger than that of the cake and transfer the paste onto a cake card. Place the cake upside down on the paste and trim any excess paste from around the edge. To do this, follow the bottom edge (which will actually be the top) of the carved cake with a sharp knife. Then flip the cake over onto the spare cake card and set aside.

26 Roll out more white sugarpaste to a thickness of 5mm (just over 1/8") and cut out a strip which is the same height as the cake and long enough to wrap around

the circumference of the cake (use a paper template as a guide if needed). Texture the paste by pressing it with a new, hard-bristled brush.

27 Place the strip around the cake and press into the carved edges to shape. Trim away the excess and smooth out the paste at the join around the top of the cake.

28 With any leftover trimmings, roll sausages into twigs and root shapes. Glue them to the trunk with a little edible glue and texture with the back of a paintbrush. Roll sausages of paste into scroll shapes to make roots that appear as if they are coming out of the board. Allow to dry on a flat surface. Paint with Bulrush liquid food colour and allow to dry again.

COLOURING THE TREE STUMP

29 To colour the tree stump you can either use an airbrush or the splashing technique as explained on page 47. If using an airbrush, evenly apply a thin layer of Daffodil liquid food colour diluted with a few drops of cooled, boiled water, all over the piece. Airbrush the bottom end with Chestnut liquid food colour, fading the colour as you move upwards. To give extra depth, you can airbrush a third layer of Bulrush liquid food colour onto the bottom edge of the cake and into the crevices of the paste.

30 If using a toothbrush, colour the sugarpaste with Daffodil paste food colour and cover the cake as explained in points 25, 26 and 27 above. Only colour the paste if you are

using this technique, so that you are able to achieve an even colour all over the piece. Flick a thin layer of Chestnut liquid colour onto the bottom end, fading the colour as you move upwards with the toothbrush.

TUTOR TIP

When splashing colour onto the piece, try to use paste food colour diluted to the consistency that you need. It's easier to adjust the consistency of paste food colours than it is with liquid food colours.

31 Once the trunk has been coloured, use a palette knife to lift it with the cake card underneath and stick it to the board with either the cake filling or a dab of royal icing. I prefer to use a cake card to lift the cake

but feel free to remove it if you do not need it.

32 To cover the board, roll out pieces of sugarpaste coloured with Daffodil and a touch of Teddy Bear Brown paste colours to a thickness of 3mm ($^1/_8$"). Glue to the board with a little edible glue and texture by pressing and tearing the paste with the tip of a star nozzle.

FINISHING TOUCHES

33 Dust the feet, ears and hands of the fairy with Daffodil dust food colour, making sure you evenly blend the colour. Glue down the roots that will stick out of the cake board with a dot of softened paste. Glue the butterflies onto the tree stump and

board so that they look pleasing to the eye.

ASSEMBLY

34 Transport the fairy figure to the venue in a separate box, as explained on page 48, then glue it onto the cake with a dot of royal icing.

TUTOR TIP

If you need more servings, you can make the trunk out of a carved dummy covered with paste which can be used as a base whilst building the fairy. Make a round cake that will serve as many people as you need, then place the whole piece onto the cake. This method also means that you can keep the fairy and tree stump as a memento.

Mint marshmallow treats

To make these biscuits, follow the recipe on page 16 for the chocolate flavour and use a small, round cutter to ensure they are all the same size.

Add a few drops of green liquid food colour and a few drops of mint extract to the marshmallow recipe on page 23 then pipe mint marshmallow onto each biscuit. To make them even more delicious I love to pipe chocolate ganache into the centre of the biscuit before adding the swirl of mint marshmallow on top and around the chocolate ganache centre.

Sprinkle each biscuit with desiccated coconut coloured with green food colour and decorate with butterflies made from Black SFP.

I came up with this idea after living in an old house in Edinburgh where I would often find mice in the kitchen. The mice were as cute as the ones I have made in this scene but of course I couldn't let them stay!

I created this centrepiece with an individual cake and a pastillage cup. The mini cakes can be arranged on the presentation table with mice among the cups and sweets.

THE QUEST FOR FOOD

EDIBLES

Twelve 7cm diameter x 5cm tall (2¾" x 2") round mini cakes (see page 39)

1.5kg (3lb 5oz) SK Marzipan (optional)

Sugarpaste/rolled fondant: 2.15kg (4lb 12oz) white

SK Instant Mix Pastillage: 200g (7oz) pale pink (coloured with a touch of Poinsettia (red) and a touch of Daffodil (yellow) Professional Paste Food Colours), 50g (1¾oz) white (uncoloured)

SK Sugar Florist Paste (SFP)/gum paste: 400g (14oz) White

SK Professional Paste Food Colours: Blackberry, Cyclamen, Daffodil, Edelweiss (white), Fuchsia, Poinsettia (Christmas red), Teddy Bear Brown

SK Professional Dust Food Colour: Chestnut

SK Designer Pastel Dust Food Colour: Pastel Pink

SK Designer Dust Food Colour: Etruscan Brick

SK Professional Liquid Food Colours: Chestnut, Holly/Ivy, Jet Black

SK Instant Mix Royal Icing: 100g (3½oz)

Orange liqueur or other clear alcohol

Sugar cubes

EQUIPMENT

Basic equipment (see page 6)

23cm (9") square cake drum/board

12 x 7cm (2¾") round cake cards

7.5cm (3") diameter round former (e.g. plastic tube or a food tin covered with thin cardboard)

5cm and 7cm (2" and 2¾") round cutters

Fluted edge cutter

15mm (⅝") width ribbon: white

Templates (see page 183)

CAKE BOARD

1   Colour 150g (5¼oz) of white sugarpaste light Teddy Bear Brown, roll out to a thickness of 3mm (⅛") and cover the square cake drum. Rub a smoother over the paste to remove any imperfections then trim the excess paste from the edges with a plain-bladed knife. Glue the white ribbon onto the side of the board with a non-toxic glue stick and set aside.

LINEN CLOTH

2   Lightly grease a non-stick board with white vegetable fat then thinly roll out 100g (3½oz) of White SFP into a rectangle measuring approximately 30cm x 23cm (12" x 9"). Trim the edges with a fluted edge cutter. To make the lace pattern, cut out a variety of shapes using a teardrop shape cutter, a small round cutter and a leaf cutter as shown. Arrange the pattern on one corner of the cloth. Place the cloth on the board, create a few pleats on one side and leave the opposite side flat.

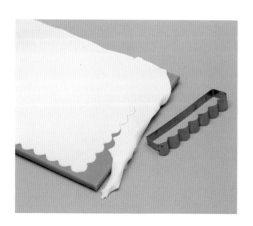

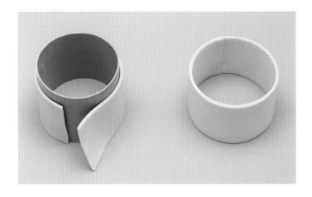

3   Make up some royal icing to soft-peak consistency to make the line work (see page 27). Fill a small piping bag with the royal icing and snip off the very end, or place a no. 2 nozzle in the bag before filling with icing. Pipe a line onto the outer edge of the linen cloth, following the fluted design. Add a second, inner line and pipe small dots to complete the edge work. To create the lace effect, pipe criss-cross lines of royal icing within the cut-out shapes then add scrolls to complete the design.

PASTILLAGE CUP

4   Roll some pale pink pastillage to a thickness of 3mm (^{1}/$_8$") on a non-stick board and cut out a strip for the cup using a paper template. Place the strip around the 7.5cm (3") round plastic tube (or a food tin covered with thin card). Trim the ends if needed and smooth the joins

by pressing them together gently. Once the paste has firmed remove the former and let it dry completely.

5   To make the bottom of the cup, brush edible glue onto the bottom edge of the cylinder. Roll out some pale pink pastillage to a thickness of 3mm (^{1}/$_8$") and gently press the cylinder onto the paste. Cut neatly around the base using a sharp knife then set aside to dry completely.

6   To decorate the cup, thinly roll out a small piece of pale Fuchsia-coloured SFP. Roll a tiny piece of pale Cyclamen SFP into a ball and press gently onto the paste. Roll over with the rolling pin to merge the two colours and cut out a flower shape using a daisy cutter. Attach the flower to the side of the cup with edible glue.

7   To make the handle, roll some pale pink pastillage into a thin sausage and curve into a scroll shape, using the template provided as a guide. You need to make twelve handles if you are making the mini cakes.

8   To make the base of the cup, roll some pale pink pastillage into a sausage 1cm (^{3}/$_8$") thick and wrap it around a 5cm (2") round cutter to make the ring shape. Trim the excess paste and smooth the joins by pressing them gently. Remove the cutter and allow to dry completely.

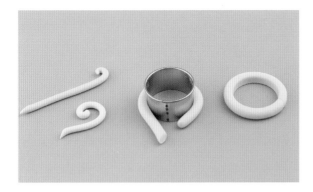

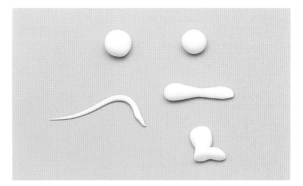

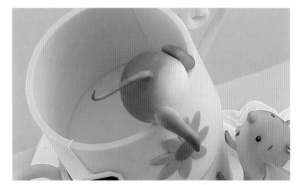

Make two for the cake or, if you are making the mini cakes, make twelve altogether.

9 Once the base and handle are fully dry, glue them to the pastillage cup with some pale pink royal icing in a small paper piping bag. Hold the handle in position with a piece of polystyrene until fully dry.

TUTOR TIP

I have made this piece of work before with two pastillage cups on top of the mini cake instead of one. Adding two cups will give height to the centrepiece and create a focal point, ideal if you are making this for a big celebration. Try decorating the cups with different patterns for a more unique effect.

MOUSE IN THE CUP

TUTOR TIP

You can make the mice with marzipan instead of flowerpaste if you would like to give them as souvenirs or as a nice treat, or just for those who love marzipan.

10 To make the body, roll a ball of White SFP into a pear shape and trim the narrow end. To hold the mouse in the required position, place a piece of polystyrene into the pastillage cup. Push the body of the mouse into a cocktail stick to hold it upright. Press it gently towards the rim of the cup, leaving the mouse's bottom sticking out.

11 To make the bent leg, roll a small piece of White SFP into a thin bottle shape. Bend at the thinner end to create the foot. Pinch to bring out the heel and to give shape to the foot. Glue to the right side of the body with edible glue and shape the foot around the rim of the cup.

TUTOR TIP

Do not glue the foot to the rim of the cup yet as the body has to be removed from the cup for dusting. Just use the rim to place the leg and foot into the required position.

12 Make the left leg in the same way and glue to the body in a straight position.

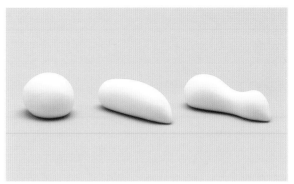

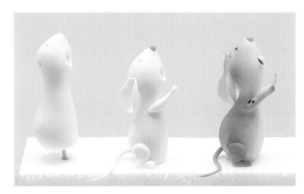

13 For the tail, roll a thin sausage of White SFP and leave to dry. When dry, push the tail into the body (the body should still be soft inside at this point), and secure with a little edible glue. Once dry, remove the mouse and the piece of polystyrene from the cup. Leave the cocktail stick inside the body of the mouse to help you hold it while you dust it.

14 Using a soft brush, brush the back, tail and feet with Chestnut dust food colour. To control the colour, blot any excess dust onto a piece of kitchen paper first then dust the mouse until the desired shade has been achieved. Leave the mouse's belly colour-free. Once the mouse is finished, remove the cocktail stick and glue to the pastillage cup in the required position with a dot of softened pastillage.

STANDING MOUSE

15 Roll 50g (1¾oz) of White SFP into a ball, then roll this into a sausage with a pointed end. Stroke the paste towards the pointed end to create the head and neck. At this point, push a skewer ¾ of the way into the paste to support the body.

TUTOR TIP

When inserting the skewer into the body, make sure you push and twist it at the same time. Insert the skewer into about ⅔ of the length of the body to avoid deforming the piece. As the skewer is only used to hold the shape of the body temporarily, grease the skewer with vegetable fat so it can be removed easily later on.

16 Open the mouse's mouth with the end of a paintbrush, then open the eye sockets with a cocktail stick. To insert the ears, make holes on each side of the head so that you know where the ears will be placed. Allow the body to firm in an upright position on a piece of polystyrene.

17 Make the tail and feet as explained before. Glue to the body in the required position with a little edible glue.

18 For the arms, roll a small ball of White SFP into a thin bottle shape. Flatten the smaller end to create the hand and glue to the body so that it is in a leaning position, as shown.

19 For the nose, roll a tiny piece of pale pink SFP into a teardrop shape. Glue to the pointed end of the head with a little edible glue.

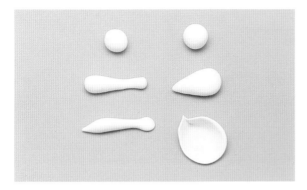

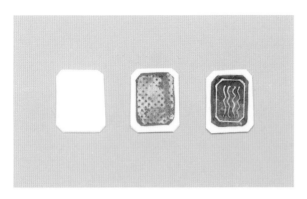

20 For the ears, roll a tiny ball of White SFP into a teardrop shape and flatten it down with a small rolling pin. Press a small ball tool into the ears to give them shape and pinch the pointed end. Glue the pointed end to the head with a little edible glue.

21 For the hair, roll thin, pointed sausages of White SFP and glue them to the head of the mouse, ensuring that they are slightly curled.

22 Once completely dry, dust the body with Chestnut dust food colour, excluding the belly. Fill the eye sockets with a dot of Jet Black-coloured royal icing. When dry, use the tip of a cocktail stick to paint a white dot of Edelweiss paste food colour onto the black dot to give the eye expression.

23 Roll a tiny piece of Cyclamen-coloured SFP and push it into the mouth to give it depth. For the front teeth, thinly roll out a little piece of White SFP and cut out a tiny rectangle shape. Make a mark down the middle with a knife and glue to the mouth. Dust the inner part of the ears with Pastel Pink dust.

SEATED MOUSE

24 Make the body as explained for the standing mouse then skewer the body onto a piece of polystyrene and bring the pointed end (i.e. the snout) forward. To make the smile, push a small round cutter into the lower half of the face. Use the end of a paintbrush to open up the mouth directly below the smile. Open the eye sockets with a cocktail stick and set aside to firm.

25 Make the tail, legs, arms, ears and hair as explained before and glue to the body in the position required. When you are positioning the arms and making the facial details, remember that this seated mouse is holding and eating a piece of sugar cube.

26 Once dry, dust with Etruscan Brick dust food colour, again leaving the belly colour-free. Dust the inner part of the ears and cheeks with Pastel Pink dust food colour. Use a fine paintbrush and Chestnut liquid food colour to paint thin lines for the eyebrows above each eye on this mouse and the standing mouse.

TEA BAG LABEL

27 Thinly roll out a small piece of White SFP and cut out a rectangle shape to make the tea-bag label. Cut off the corners and set aside.

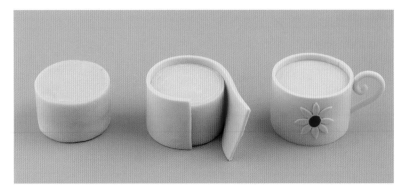

28 Use Holly/Ivy liquid food colour and a fine paintbrush to paint a smaller rectangle onto the paste, then place a piece of kitchen paper onto the fresh paint to remove some of the liquid food colour. When dry, pipe wavy lines with Daffodil-coloured royal icing onto the label.

29 Once dry, glue the label to the side of the cup with a piece of softened pastillage, or a dot of royal icing. Pipe a line of white royal icing onto the cup to make the string.

TUTOR TIP

You can personalize the mini cake cup by piping the initials of the person's name onto the label.

MINI CAKE

30 Fill and crumb-coat a mini cake, then cover the top and sides following the instructions for covering a straight-edged cake with marzipan on page 36. If marzipan is not to your taste, cover the top of the mini cake only with sugarpaste coloured with a touch of Teddy Bear Brown food colour to achieve a 'tea with milk' shade. Remember to stick a small cake card underneath when you turn it the right way up.

31 To decorate the side of the mini cake roll some pale pink sugarpaste to a thickness of 3mm (1/8") and cut out a strip 1cm (3/8") higher than the actual depth of the cake. Brush the marzipan layer with orange liqueur or clear alcohol (omit this part if you have not used marzipan) then place the pink strip

around the mini cake and trim the excess paste at the join. Leave the paste to firm.

32 Glue on the handle with royal icing and support it with a piece of polystyrene until fully dry. Finish with a flower as described for the pastillage cup. Using royal icing, glue the mini cake to the pastillage ring base. (Remember that the cake card under the mini cake will act as a support).

ASSEMBLY

33 Glue the mini cake to the board with royal icing. Place the pastillage cup with the mouse slightly tilted to one side as shown in the picture. Secure the pastillage cup to the mini cake with a dot of royal icing. Arrange and stick the mice onto

the board with a dot of soft royal icing.
Scatter pieces of sugar cube all over
the cake board.

34 For long-distance
transportation, place the
pastillage cup with the mouse in a
separate box then position it on the
board upon arrival at the venue.

Mini-cup treats

Create these cute cups following the same
method as explained in the main project. You can
vary the colour and design to match real cups
and saucers that you may already have at home.
Place the mini cakes onto the real saucers to
surprise your guests with an edible cup!

For a fun, playful touch, cut out a 'steam'
silhouette from rice paper and glue it to the top of
the minicake with a dot of edible glue.

FASHIONISTA

This beautiful young trend-setter sets out without a care in the world. It looks as if the clothes were made only for her and no-one else – all eyes are on her but she doesn't even notice.

Square or round cake for the servings required, filled and covered with white sugarpaste (see pages 32 to 34)

Sugarpaste/rolled fondant: 400g (14oz) white (plus white sugarpaste for the cake and board covering)

SK Sugar Florist Paste (SFP)/gum paste: 50g (1¾oz) coloured dark Berberis, 200g (7oz) coloured a pale skin tone with a touch of Teddy Bear Brown, 100g (3½oz) Violet, 100g (3½oz) White

SK Professional Paste Food Colours: Berberis, Fuchsia, Hydrangea, Poppy, Teddy Bear Brown, Violet

SK Professional Dust Food Colour: Violet

SK Designer Pastel Dust Food Colour: Pastel Pink

SK Professional Liquid Food Colour: Chestnut

SK Instant Mix Royal Icing: 50g (1¾oz)

Equipment

Basic equipment (see page 6)
Cake drum/board 5cm (2") bigger than the cake
Cake card the same shape and size as the cake
7cm (2¾") square x 8cm (3⅛") deep polystyrene dummy (or a size and shape to suit your cake), plus polystyrene pieces for support
Piping nozzle: no. 1
Food-grade foam sponge pieces
15mm (⅝") width ribbon: violet
Templates (see page 184)

Girl

Legs

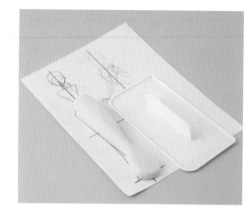

1 Divide 200g (7oz) of White SFP coloured with a touch of Teddy Bear Brown paste food colour in half and seal half the paste in a food-grade plastic bag for later. Roll 100g (3½oz) of the paste into a sausage for the legs, using the template as a guide to determine the width and length of the sausage. Stroke the paste from the waist down to thin it out and leave a piece of paste at the end, as if making a mermaid's tail.

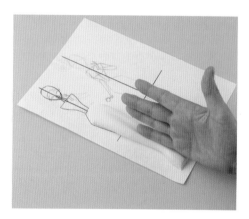

2 Flatten the paste down by pressing a smoother onto the paste or by rubbing it with the palm of your hand. Try to make the paste thicker at the waist end and thinner at the feet end. Trim the excess paste from the top and bottom, following the template as a guide. Lightly press the paste along the middle to create a groove, representing the two legs.

3 Push a skewer into the bottom end of the paste up to the knees, twist the upper part of the paste and leave the bottom end flat as shown. Bend slightly at the knees and set aside to dry on its side. Once dry, skewer the legs into a dummy so that you can build the rest of the figure.

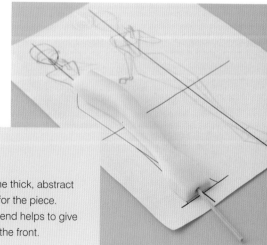

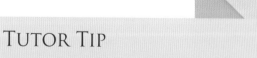

Tutor Tip

At first sight this piece looks fragile, but the thick, abstract shape of the legs makes a solid support for the piece. Twisting the legs slightly from the bottom end helps to give the piece a slender look when seen from the front.

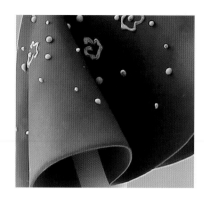
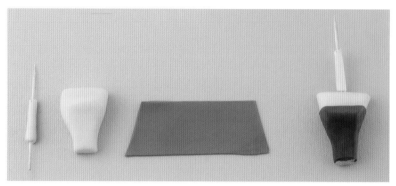

Skirt

4   For the skirt, roll out some Violet SFP on a non-stick board that has been greased with white vegetable fat. Cut out a circle using the template provided. Dust the surface of one side of the circle with Violet dust to brighten it, then glue it onto the waist with a little edible glue. Create pleats by folding the paste with your fingers into the position required.

5   Cover the end of a skewer with a piece of paste at the top to prevent it from tearing the paste of the skirt. Lift one side of the skirt and use the skewer and pieces of polystyrene as a support in order to give it movement. Insert a cocktail stick into the waist and set aside to dry.

Torso

6   To make the torso, roll some of the reserved White SFP coloured with a touch of Teddy Bear Brown into a bottle shape. Roll out the wider side with a small rolling pin, leaving a bump in the paste to create the chest. Trim the excess paste from both ends to create a neat edge, especially at the shoulder line so you give a trapezium shape to the piece. Insert a cocktail stick into the waist to create a hole through the paste, then remove it. Set aside to dry.

Neck

7   For the neck, roll some of the White SFP coloured with a touch of Teddy Bear Brown into a ball and push it onto a cocktail stick. Roll the paste into a thin sausage. Trim the paste to the length required, leaving a piece of cocktail stick protruding from both ends. Set aside to dry. Once dry, insert the neck in to the torso and glue it in place with softened paste.

8   To dress up the top, thinly roll out some Violet SFP and cut out a strip. Use Violet dust to enhance the colour and glue it around the torso with a little edible glue. Trim the excess paste from the back and push the torso onto the cocktail stick that you inserted

TUTOR TIP

Arranging the skirt so that it is floating out to one side gives the idea of the wind blowing and brings the figure to life.

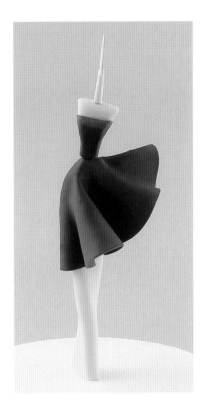

into the waist through the hole that you previously made in the torso. Glue the torso to the skirt with softened Violet SFP, making sure that it is slightly tilted to one side, and set aside to dry.

9 To make the belt, roll a tiny piece of bright Berberis-coloured SFP into a sausage and glue around the waist with a little edible glue. Trim the excess paste at the back with a pair of scissors.

Head

10 Roll some of the White SFP coloured with a touch of Teddy Bear Brown into a teardrop shape. Gently press a small round cutter onto the lower half of the paste to indent a smile. Push into the paste below the smile with a Dresden tool to bring the lower lip out. Let the head firm up before making the rest of the facial details.

11 For the nose, roll a tiny piece of paste into a teardrop shape and glue it above the mouth. Blend the thinner end of the paste into the face and pinch the wider end to turn up the nose. Use a cutting tool to give shape to the nose and trim off the excess paste if required. Use a fine paintbrush and Chestnut liquid food colour to paint the eyelashes and eyebrows.

12 To make the lips, roll a small amount of Fuchsia-coloured SFP into tiny sausages with pointed ends and glue onto the upper and lower part of the smile. Dust the cheeks and eyelids with Pastel Pink dust food colour. Once the facial details are finished, trim off the top of the head using a sharp knife where the hat will be placed and set aside to dry until it is firm enough to handle.

Hat

13 To make the hat, roll some dark Berberis-coloured SFP into a teardrop shape and glue it to the back of the head, around the sides and up to the hairline. Skewer the head into a piece of polystyrene to keep the rounded shape of the hat and leave the whole piece until it is firm enough to handle. Once dry, push it onto the cocktail stick protruding from the neck. Glue the head to the neck in the required position with a little softened paste.

14 To texture the hat, use a piping bag fitted with a no. 1 nozzle and pale orange royal icing to pipe small comma shapes all over the hat. To make the brim, colour some SFP pale orange using Berberis paste food colour, roll into a thin sausage and glue it around the edge where the hat joins the head.

15 Once the hat details are finished, make the ears from small teardrops of SFP and glue them to the sides of the hat just below the eye line. Pipe a tiny dot of white royal icing onto each ear to make earrings.

16 To make the flower on the hat, thinly roll out some of the pale orange SFP and cut out three concentric circles. Soften the edges of each circle by pressing onto the paste with a ball tool and glue one on top of the other. Pinch the circles from the back to create pleats and glue to one side of the hat with a little edible glue. Press the centre of the flower gently with a small ball tool in order to stick it firmly onto the hat.

17 To make the skirt pattern, fill a small paper piping bag with pale Violet-coloured royal icing and snip off the very end. Pipe flower shapes onto the skirt and around the waist, fading the pattern as you move down. To complete the pattern pipe orange and Hydrangea-coloured royal icing dots as shown.

Arms

18 Make the arms from the Teddy Bear Brown-coloured SFP as explained in the Ballerina project (see page 54). Glue the arms to the side of the torso as shown and support with a piece of foam sponge until they are fully dry. Glue two thin strips of Violet SFP onto the shoulders (where the arms meet the torso) to make the shoulder straps.

BAG

19 Roll a small piece of the pale orange SFP into a ball. Flatten the ball down slightly and trim the top to make a straight edge. Use a cutting tool to mark crosses all over the surface of the paste. To make the flap, roll the paste into a sausage and flatten it down. Trim one end to the length needed and create a neat, straight end. Glue this onto the top of the bag with a little edible glue. Finish with a tiny ball of red paste for the clasp and set aside to dry.

TUTOR TIP

For the bent arm it is easier to bend it and leave it on the work surface until is firm enough to handle, then glue it to the torso at the required angle.

ASSEMBLY AND FINISHING TOUCHES

20 To position the bag, first roll some of the orange SFP into a thin sausage for the handle and place it around the left arm, making sure you position it where the bag will be glued to the skirt. Glue the bag to the skirt with a little softened paste and the handle to the bag with a little edible glue.

21 To make the strips of the shoes, roll thin sausages of orange SFP and glue them to the front of the legs at an angle, as shown in the main picture. Finish by sticking tiny balls of paste to both ends of the straps for the buckles.

POLYSTYRENE BASE

22 Cover a square polystyrene dummy with white sugarpaste and set aside to dry. Glue a violet ribbon at the bottom of the base with a dot of royal icing.

23 Skewer the figure into the polystyrene base following the Tutor Tip on page 160.

24 To transport the figure, follow the instructions given in the 'Just Married' project (see pages 153 to 161). Once you arrive at your destination, glue the polystyrene dummy cake onto the real cake with a dab of royal icing then skewer the figure into the dummy cake. (There is no need to glue the figure onto the dummy as

the skewer will hold the figure in place.) It is important to use a dummy cake to keep the figure upright.

TUTOR TIP

Feel free to add any other accessories to the girl, such as a pearl necklace, a watch or a ring. If you want to avoid doing the finishing touches upon arrival, add details that are unlikely to break during transportation.

25 Before serving the cake, remove the base and the figure together. Remember that the figure contains inedible supports so must not be eaten.

FLOWER BISCUITS

Bake biscuits in the shape of flowers
following your chosen recipe (see
suggestions on page 16). Outline the
biscuits with soft-peak royal icing in a
piping bag with a no. 2 nozzle, then
flood in the shape with royal icing made
to run-out consistency. Choose colours
that match the centrepiece: for the
Fashionista cake I have chosen hues of
violet, fuchsia and yellow.

Toy cars are always popular among children, so I couldn't help including a colourful buggy to draw their attention. I decided to make an intricate design incorporating as much detail as possible, so you can choose how much work you put into your cake and simplify it if desired. Remember that you can adapt the design to make your own car cakes, using some or all of these techniques and following the child's favourite toy car as a guide.

DUNE BUGGY

EDIBLES

20cm x 15cm (8" x 6") rectangular cake

Sugarpaste/rolled fondant: 960g (2lb 2oz) white

900g (2lb) SK Instant Mix Pastillage

SK Sugar Florist Paste (SFP)/gum paste: 150g (5¼oz) Black

SK Paste Food Colours: Berberis, Cyclamen, Jet Black, Lilac, Poinsettia (Christmas red), Sunflower, Sunny Lime

SK Professional Liquid Food Colours: Blackberry, Cyclamen

100g (3½oz) SK Instant Mix Royal Icing

EQUIPMENT

Basic equipment (see page 6)

28cm (11") square cake board (optional, for presentation/ transportation)

20cm x 15cm (8" x 6") rectangular cake card

20cm x 15cm x 2cm (8" x 6" x ¾") block of polystyrene

3cm (1⅛") spacers

Sugar shaper

15mm (⅝") width ribbon: black (for cake board, see note under point 1)

Templates (see pages 184 to 187)

CAKE BOARD

1 Colour 300g (10½oz) of white sugarpaste with Lilac paste food colour to make a pale lilac tone. Roll out the sugarpaste to a thickness of 3mm (1⅛") and cover the square cake drum. Rub a smoother over the paste to remove any imperfections then trim the excess paste from around the edges with a sharp knife. Glue a length of black ribbon onto the edge of the board with a non-toxic glue stick and set aside to dry.

Note: Although this cake has not been photographed on a board, mounting the buggy on a covered board will make it easier to display and transport.

BUGGY

Chassis

2 Make up the pastillage following the instructions on the pack, then roll out to a thickness of 1cm (⅜") and cut out the chassis using the template provided. Roll out more pastillage to a thickness of 5mm (just over ⅛") and cut out the wheel axles using the template. Leave the different parts to dry completely on a flat surface dusted with cornflour.

3 Cut a piece of polystyrene 2cm (¾") deep into a trapezoid shape in order to support the weight of the cake and to help prevent the base from cracking during transportation.

Make the different parts of the buggy in advance to allow for drying time.

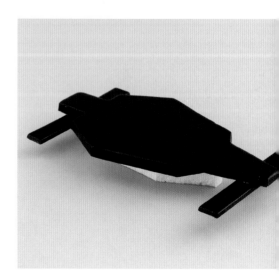

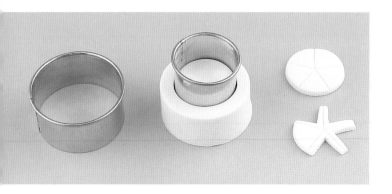

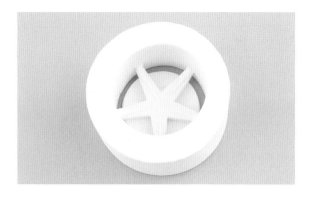

4 Once all the parts have dried, glue the wheel axles to the front and back of the chassis with royal icing on one side only. Follow the template drawings to see exactly where the axles should be placed. Glue the piece of polystyrene onto the middle of the base with royal icing; let the base dry then flip it over.

5 Paint the whole base black. Use Blackberry liquid food colour, or Jet Black paste food colour diluted with a few drops of cooled, boiled water and a medium, flat-shaped paintbrush. Let the paint dry and brush or spray the surface with confectioners' glaze to prevent the paint from staining your hands when handling the base.

Wheels

6 Roll 80g (2¾oz) of pastillage into a ball. Flatten the ball down to 3cm (1⅛") in depth using a cake smoother with 3cm (1⅛") spacers to each side to achieve an even thickness. Dust a 6.5cm (2½") round cutter with cornflour to prevent the paste from sticking and cut out the wheel. Cut out the inner part of the wheel using a 4.5cm (1¾") round cutter. Remove the centre piece and let the wheel dry on a flat surface. Make the other three wheels in the same way.

7 To make the wheel rims, roll some pastillage to a thickness of 5mm (just over ⅛") and cut out a 4.5cm (1¾") circle. Emboss five radial lines using a plain-bladed knife then cut out triangle shapes in between each line to achieve the shape required (see templates to illustrate). Make one rim at a time to prevent the pastillage from drying out while you are working (keep the rest in a sealed polythene bag). Let the four rims dry completely.

TUTOR TIP

Although pastillage is edible it dries very hard so it isn't particularly pleasant to eat. If you want to make a more palatable buggy you can replace the pastillage base with gingerbread baked in the shape of the chassis and wheel axles. Glue the pieces of gingerbread together with royal icing. To support the whole structure, layer spare pieces of gingerbread underneath to lift the chassis up to the height required instead of using polystyrene. Bake the dough well to make the dough firmer than usual as this will prevent it from cracking.

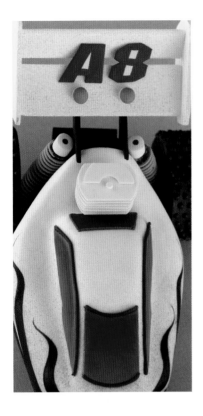

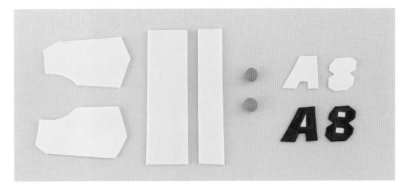

8 To glue the rims in position, roll a piece of spare pastillage to a thickness of 3mm (¹/₈") and cut out a circle smaller than the inner circle of the wheel. Place the round piece of paste at the bottom of the wheel (which will help to lift the rim by a few millimetres) then place the rim upside down onto the circle. Glue each pointed end of the rim to the inner part of the wheel using a dot of royal icing. Set aside to dry.

9 To make the tyres, fill a paper piping bag with soft-peak royal icing and snip off the very end. On the sides of the wheel, pipe dots of icing to create a tyre effect. Pipe lines of royal icing from the centre of the rim down to the sides, and set aside to dry.

10 Once the icing has dried, paint the wheels with Blackberry liquid food colour or Jet Black paste food colour diluted with a few drops of cooled, boiled water.

11 To finish, make a tiny ball of Sunny Lime-coloured pastillage and stick it onto the centre of the rim while the paint is still fresh. Once the paint has dried, paint the wheels with a thin layer of confectioners' glaze.

TUTOR TIP

The circle of paste will support the rim while it dries. If the rim doesn't fit into the wheel, softly file the ends with sandpaper to make it smaller. If the rim is smaller, fill in the gaps with some of the royal icing that you used for gluing.

Rear wing

12 Colour the remaining pastillage bright yellow using Sunflower paste food colour. Roll out the coloured pastillage to a thickness of 3mm (¹/₈") and cut out all the parts of the rear wing using the templates provided, including the lettering needed. Allow to dry.

13 Once the parts have dried, glue them together with Sunflower-coloured royal icing. To make this as easy as possible, place pieces 1 and 2 on a piece of wedge-shaped polystyrene which should help you achieve the height required. Use cocktail sticks to keep the parts in position and to stop them from sliding or moving whilst they dry. Leave to dry.

14 Paint the letter 'A' and the number '8' using a fine paintbrush and Cyclamen liquid food

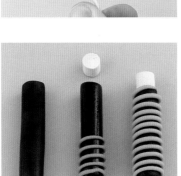

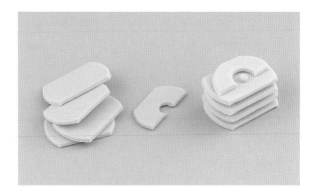

colour (or Cyclamen paste diluted with a few drops of cooled, boiled water), using the template as a guide. (Alternatively, make your own letters and numerals to suit the recipient.) Make two tiny hemispheres from Poinsettia-coloured sugarpaste to decorate the rear wing. Glue the letter, number and hemispheres on the rear wing with dots of royal icing.

Suspension

15 Roll some Black SFP into a long sausage approximately 1cm (³/₈") wide. Cut out four 6cm (2³/₈") long segments and insert a cocktail stick greased with white vegetable fat into one end. Stick the sausages into a piece of polystyrene in an upright position to avoid the sides going flat and allow to firm up.

16 To make the springs, fit a sugar shaper with a 2mm (¹/₈") round-hole disc. Colour 50g (1¾oz) of White SFP a soft grey shade, add a little white vegetable fat and place it in the sugar shaper. Brush each black sausage with a little edible glue and pipe a thin line of paste onto it while spinning it at the same time to make a spiral. Once completed, push the stick into a piece of polystyrene and let it stand upright until fully dry. To finish, roll a little Sunny Lime-coloured SFP into a sausage and split into four pieces, each 1cm (³/₈") long. Glue onto

the top end of each spring with a little edible glue. Set aside to dry.

Engine intake

17 Thinly roll out some Sunny Lime-coloured SFP and cut out the pieces for the engine intake using the templates provided. Let them dry, pile them up and stick all the pieces together with a tiny ball of softened paste, ensuring to leave a gap in between. Set aside to dry.

TUTOR TIPS

If you don't have a sugar shaper, fill a paper piping bag with firm-peak grey-coloured royal icing and snip off the end to make a 2mm (¹/₈") hole. Pipe a thin line all around the sausage while turning it at the same time to make the spring.

You can make the engine intake out of one piece of paste for quicker modelling. Mark horizontal lines on the sides with a plain-bladed knife to give the detail required.

Front and rear wing

18 Cut out all the pieces for the front and rear wing from Black SFP rolled to the thickness required using the templates provided. Cut out two of template A with a thickness of 3mm (1/8") and leave to dry on a rolling pin to curve. Cut out two of template E and two of D to a thickness of 5mm (just over 1/8"). Cut out template F to a thickness of 1cm (3/8"). Cut out template B to a thickness of 1.5cm (5/8"). Cut out template C to a thickness of 3cm (1 1/8").

19 Allow all the different parts to dry completely before assembling. Glue the rear wing pieces together with dots of royal icing, following the guidelines provided on the templates as a reference.

CAKE

20 To carve the car shape, make a chassis paper template slightly smaller than the one provided and place it on top of the rectangular cake. Trim the sides of the cake with a serrated knife following the template. Next, make a perpendicular curved cut from the back to the top of the cake, leaving the back higher than the opposite end.

21 To make the cockpit, use the trimmings of the cake and cut out a wedge shape, as shown. Cut the cake into two layers then fill and crumb-coat with buttercream or ganache. Stick the cake onto a rectangular cake card cut into the shape of the chassis with a dab of the filling then chill in the fridge for a couple of hours.

22 To cover the cake, roll out 500g (1lb 1¾oz) of Sunflower-coloured sugarpaste to a thickness of 5mm (just over 1/8"). Place the paste on top of the cake and rub it gently with the palm of your hand to smooth out the pleats and give shape. Trim the excess paste at the bottom edge using a plain-bladed knife.

23 Flick colour onto the front wing of the car using a new toothbrush and Berberis paste food colour diluted with a few drops of cooled, boiled water (see page 47). Try to fade the drops of colour towards the back wing, creating a focal point of colour at the front.

24 To make the side windows and windscreen, thinly roll out some Cyclamen-coloured sugarpaste and cut out the shapes using the template provided as a guide. Glue the windows and windscreen to the cockpit with a little edible glue. Make the back window using the windscreen

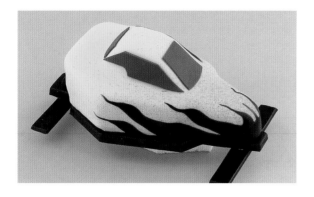

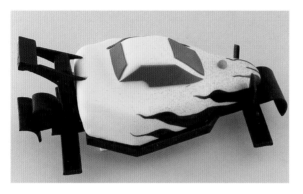

template as reference and trim to the size needed.

25 Paint flames onto the front and sides of the cake using a fine paintbrush and Blackberry liquid food colour or black paste food colour diluted with a few drops of cooled, boiled water to the consistency of gouache paint. If you are not confident enough to paint, thinly roll out some Black SFP and cut out flames using a paper template as a guide if needed. Attach the flames to the buggy with edible glue. Remember to turn the template over when you cut flames for the opposite side in order to create a symmetrical design.

ASSEMBLY AND FINISHING TOUCHES

26 Glue the front and rear wing pieces onto the pastillage base with dots of stiff royal icing and use spare pieces of Black SFP to give support (especially for pieces D and A). Make sure you secure the piece that supports the rear wing to the cake with stiff royal icing or softened pastillage to give the support required. Allow to dry.

27 Glue the engine intake right at the back of the cockpit. Glue a tiny hemisphere of Poinsettia-coloured sugarpaste to the front. Pipe lines of dark Cyclamen-coloured royal icing onto the edges of the window to give a neat finish. Stick the car's polystyrene support onto the board with a dab of royal icing.

28 Glue the wheel to the top end of the axles with a dot of royal icing. Remove the excess icing with a clean brush to give a neat finish. (I have used white icing to show this clearly in the picture, however you can use black icing for a neater finish.)

29 Glue the suspension pieces to the front and rear wheel axles with a dot of softened, black-coloured sugarpaste. Let the suspension lean onto the cake to give it support and prevent it from sliding down the cake during transportation. Finally, glue the rear wing onto the support at the back with royal icing. Although it is quite safe to transport, you can glue the rear wing to its support upon arrival at the venue if preferred.

30 Place the cake onto the covered board and secure with a little royal icing.

Dune Buggy Biscuits

Layer three biscuits with chocolate ganache or buttercream. Smooth out the sides of the biscuits and chill in the fridge until the filling has set.

Cover the top with a thin layer of black-coloured sugarpaste.

Make the rims as explained in the dune buggy project and paint with SK Silver Edible Paint. Glue the rim on top of the biscuits, trim the ends if required and then cover the side with a strip of paste slightly higher than the biscuits.

Pipe black dots around the sides and allow to dry. Glue a small cylinder of Sunflower-coloured sugarpaste or SFP onto the centre, press a small ball tool into it and pipe a dot of black royal icing to finish.

Once dry, you can arrange the wheels on the presentation table around the main cake or just wrap them individually as a treat.

In this project I tried to re-create the memory I have of my granny, my sister and my brother making a cake together in my granny's hometown, Máximo Paz. The cake had to be made under her strict supervision so we wouldn't forget any of the steps required to ensure its success. I still remember the smell of her walnut cake baking in the oven which was to be finished with a lovely rich buttercream filling and a creamy chocolate coating. My mum was keener on eating the cake than helping!

GRANNY'S KITCHEN

EDIBLES

11cm (4½") x 9cm (3½") deep dome-shaped cake, filled and crumb-coated with buttercream (or any other filling of your choice)

Sugarpaste/rolled fondant: 250g (8¾oz) white coloured with Terracotta, 350g (12¼oz) white coloured with Teddy Bear Brown

SK Instant Mix Pastillage: 200g (7oz) coloured with pale Teddy Bear Brown, 50g (1¾oz) white (uncoloured)

SK Mexican Modelling Paste (MMP): 80g (2¾oz) Cream Celebration, 150g (5¼oz) Soft Beige, 530g (1lb 2¾oz) White

SK Paste Food Colours: Berberis, Bulrush, Dark Forest, Edelweiss (white), Hyacinth, Jet Black, Olive, Poppy, Rose, Sunflower, Teddy Bear Brown, Terracotta, Wisteria

SK Designer Pastel Dust Food Colour: Pastel Pink

SK Designer Metallic Lustre Dust Food Colour: Copper

SK Professional Liquid Food Colours: Chestnut, Holly/Ivy, Hyacinth, Poppy, Rose, Sunflower, Wisteria (or the same paste food colours diluted with a few drops of cooled, boiled water to a watercolour consistency)

EQUIPMENT

Basic equipment (see page 6)

28cm (11") square cake drum/board

10cm (4") round cake card

5cm (2") polystyrene hemisphere former

15mm (⅝") width ribbon: pale gold

Templates (see page 187)

CAKE BOARD

1 Roll out 350g (12¼oz) of Teddy Bear Brown-coloured sugarpaste to a thickness of 3mm (⅛") and cover the square cake drum. Rub a cake smoother over the paste to achieve an even surface then trim the excess paste from the edges with a plain-bladed knife.

2 Emboss lines with the edge of a ruler to make the floor tiles. Add some texture by flicking Chestnut liquid food colour diluted with a few drops of cooled, boiled water using a toothbrush (see page 47). Glue pale gold ribbon around the side of the board with a non-toxic glue stick to finish. Set aside to dry.

TUTOR TIP

Make the pastillage pieces for the table and chair in advance to allow for drying time.

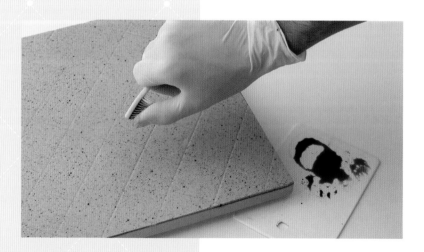

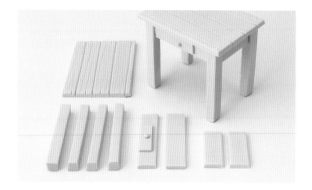

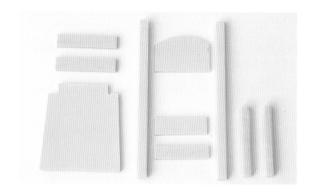

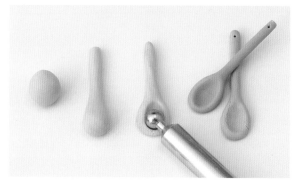

TABLE PIECES

3 To make the table, roll out some pale Teddy Bear Brown-coloured pastillage to the thickness required for each separate part and cut out the shapes following the templates provided. Roll to a thickness of 0.5cm (just over $^1/_8$") and cut out a tabletop, two long beams and two short beams. Roll out to 1cm ($^3/_8$") and cut out four legs. Finally, roll to 3mm ($^1/_8$") and cut out one drawer. While working with pastillage remember to keep the paste sealed to prevent it from drying out. Allow all the pieces to dry thoroughly on a flat surface dusted with cornflour.

CHAIR

4 Roll out some pale Teddy Bear Brown pastillage to the thickness required for each part of the chair and cut out each piece following the

templates provided. Roll to a thickness of 5mm (just over $^1/_8$") and cut out the seat, two front legs and two back legs. Roll to 3mm ($^1/_8$") and cut two each of the upper front and side beams and the lower beams, and one chair back. Allow the pieces to dry.

COPPER BOWL

5 Thinly roll out a small piece of pastillage. To make a bowl shape, place the paste gently into an egg cup or plastic mould (I use the plastic egg tray from the fridge) that has been dusted with cornflour. Press the paste gently into the shape, smoothing out the pleats. Trim off the excess paste with a sharp knife then set aside to dry. Once dry, remove from the former.

6 To make the handle, roll a thin piece of pastillage and make a 'u' shape. Glue the handle to the bowl

with a little edible glue and set aside to dry. Paint the bowl with Copper metallic food dust diluted with a few drops of clear alcohol. Set aside to dry once more.

WOODEN SPOON

7 Roll a small amount of pale Teddy Bear Brown sugarpaste into a ball. Roll one side of the ball into a sausage to make a spoon shape then indent the rounded piece of paste at the end with a small ball tool. Set aside to dry.

ASSEMBLING AND PAINTING THE TABLE AND CHAIR

8 Once all the table pieces are dry, place the top of the table upside down and glue each part onto the

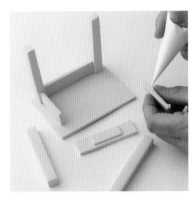

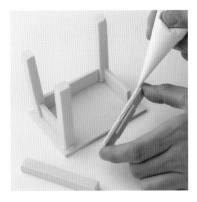

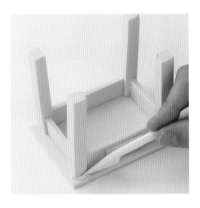

TUTOR TIP

Before gluing each piece of pastillage, position them on the underside of the table top to give you an idea where each piece is to be placed. Lift each piece one by one and glue into position. Remove the excess icing with the tip of a modelling tool then set aside to dry.

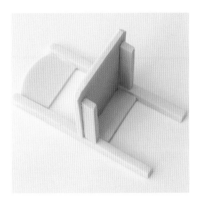

underside using a paper piping bag filled with royal icing.

9 To assemble the chair, lay it on its back as shown in the picture. Glue the pieces together with soft royal icing in the same way as for the table. Clean the excess icing off the joins and set aside to dry.

10 To paint the table and chair, use a medium flat-bristle brush and Chestnut liquid food colour (or Chestnut paste diluted with a few drops of cooled, boiled water to a watercolour consistency). Apply a thin coat of paint evenly all over the table and chair and leave to dry.

CAKE STAND

11 Thinly roll the white pastillage and cut out a circle with a

5cm (2") round cutter. Emboss an inner circle onto the paste using the blunt side of a round cutter. Place it upside down on a polystyrene hemisphere former to give it shape and allow to dry.

12 To make the stand, roll a piece of paste into a cone and trim the ends to form a trapezium shape 1.5cm ($^5/_8$") long. Glue this centrally to the underside of the circle with edible glue and leave to dry upside down on the former. When dry, paint a design on the base with a fine paintbrush and Hyacinth liquid food colour.

TUTOR TIP

You can use a fine Blue food colour pen to decorate the stand if you prefer.

LITTLE CAKE

13 Roll out the remaining pale Teddy Bear Brown pastillage to a thickness of 5mm (just over $^1/_8$") and cut out three 3.5cm (1$^3/_8$") circles using a round cutter. Allow them to firm. Fill a small piping bag with Bulrush-coloured soft royal icing and snip off the end. Layer and glue the circles together with a dot of royal icing piped on each circle.

14 Ice the little cake with some royal icing coloured with Chestnut liquid food colour. Pipe onto the top and let some of the icing run over the sides to achieve a realistic topping effect. Finish the cake with a tiny ball of Poppy-coloured paste to make the cherry on top. Glue it to the icing while it is still soft. Set aside to dry.

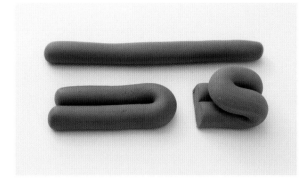

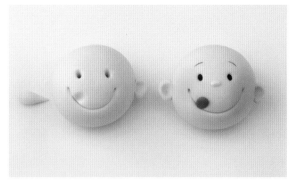

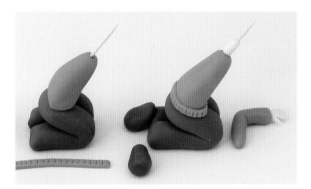

GRANDSON

Body and legs

15 To make the trousers, roll 30g (1oz) of Wisteria-coloured MMP into a sausage 1.5cm (⁵/₈") wide and fold in half to make a pair of legs. Lift the folded end and fold in half again to create a kneeling position. Set aside to dry overnight.

16 To make the torso, roll 20g (¾oz) of Hyacinth-coloured MMP into a cone, then flatten it down and glue to the trousers with a little edible glue. Cut out a strip of the same colour and glue it to the bottom end of the torso to make the waistband. Mark along the strip with a modelling tool.

17 For the neck, roll a tiny piece of Soft Beige MMP into a sausage and glue this onto the top of the torso. Push a cocktail stick through the neck and torso, leaving a piece of the stick protruding to support the head later.

18 To make the shoes, roll a small piece of Bulrush MMP into a sausage and divide it in half. Roll each piece into a pear shape and glue onto the legs with a little edible glue. Set aside to dry.

Head

19 Roll 30g (1oz) of Soft Beige MMP into a ball. For the smile, push a small round cutter into the lower half of the face. Make the dimples on either end of the smile using the tip of a cocktail stick. Push a small ball tool above the smile indentation to make room for the tongue sticking out of the mouth.

20 Using the tip of a cocktail stick, open the eye sockets along an imaginary line across the middle of the face. Fill the sockets with some piped Jet Black-coloured royal icing. When dry, paint two tiny dots of Edelweiss paste food colour onto the eyes to highlight them.

TUTOR TIP

When piping the royal icing into the eye sockets, try not to overfill them or the eyes will pop out and give the character a slightly strange look! Aim to pipe the royal icing so it is levelled with the paste. You could alternatively draw the eyes on with a Black food colour pen for a quicker finish.

21 For the ears, follow the eye line to make a hole on each

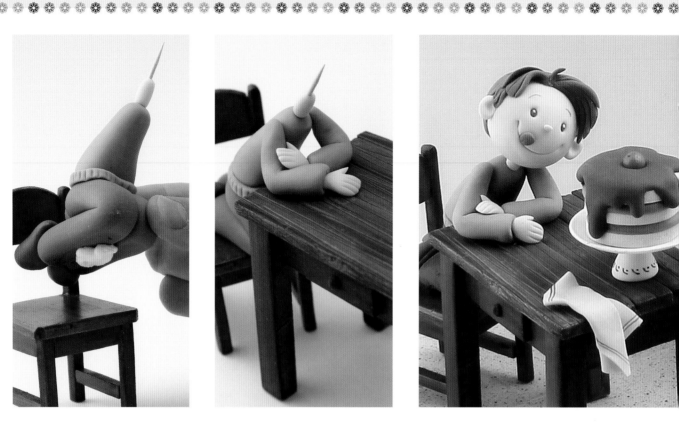

side of the head. Roll two tiny pieces of paste into teardrop shapes and stick them into the sockets with a little edible glue. Press a small ball tool into each ear. For the nose, roll a tiny piece of paste into an oval shape. Glue this below the eyes and in the middle of the face. Dust the cheeks with Pastel Pink dust food colour.

22 For the tongue, roll a tiny piece of Terracotta-coloured sugarpaste into a teardrop and glue onto the smile with a little edible glue. Paint on the eyebrows using a fine paintbrush and Chestnut liquid food colour. Leave the head to firm up.

23 To make the hair colour some MMP with Bulrush and a touch of Berberis paste food colour, roll into a teardrop shape and glue to the back of the head with a little edible glue. Bring the paste up to the forehead line and to

the back of the ears. Make indentations on the hair with the back of a knife or a modelling tool to give texture. Leave the head attached to a cocktail stick and place in a polystyrene block until needed.

24 Before making the sleeves, stick the boy onto the chair with a dot of royal icing. Position the table towards the boy's stomach to give you an idea of how to position the arms.

Arms and hands

25 For the sleeves, roll some Hyacinth-coloured MMP into a sausage and divide it in half. Narrow one end of each piece slightly then push a small ball tool into the wider end for the hands to be inserted into later on. Mark halfway along the sleeves and bend both into right angles. Glue the

sleeves to the torso with a little edible glue in the position shown.

TUTOR TIP

Do not glue the sleeves onto the table in case you have to move or rearrange the items on the board. The table will give support to the arms until they dry in the right position.

26 Roll a small piece of Soft Beige MMP into a sausage and divide it in half. Roll each piece into a long bottleneck, leaving a tiny piece of paste at the end for the hand. Flatten the hands and cut a 'v' shape out of each with small scissors to create a thumb. Make three marks to indent the fingers. To insert the hands, trim the excess paste from the wrists then

glue them to the sleeves in the position required with a little edible glue.

27 Finally, push the head into the cocktail stick sticking out of the neck and position it on the neck. To finish, make the fringe with the same paste used for the hair.

TUTOR TIP

As all the elements of this scene interact with each other, I usually attach the boy's head once the rest of the elements on the table are in place. By doing this, I know how to position the head and in which direction the character is looking. Secure the head to the neck later on with a little piece of softened paste.

GRANDDAUGHTER

Body

28 To make the long dress, roll 60g–70g (2oz–2½oz) of Dark Forest-coloured MMP into a cone 9.5cm (3¼") long. For the neck, roll some Soft Beige MMP into a sausage and glue onto the top of the cone. Push a cocktail stick into the neck and torso and leave the cone to dry on its base.

29 For the apron, thinly roll some pale Wisteria-coloured MMP and cut out a long trapezium shape. Glue to the front of the cone with edible glue. Cut strips from the trimmings to make the apron ties for the waist and neck. Decorate the bottom end of the cone with a strip of Olive-coloured MMP. Paint tiny flowers and leaves onto the apron with a fine paintbrush using Holly/Ivy and Wisteria liquid food colours.

30 Make the sleeves from Dark Forest MMP as explained for the grandson. Glue them to the sides and front of the torso with a little edible glue.

31 Make the hands as explained for the grandson and glue them to the sleeves with edible glue, placing one hand on top of the other.

Head

32 Roll 30g (1oz) of Soft Beige MMP into a rounded teardrop shape. Mark a smile and dimples as for the grandson. Open the mouth by pushing a small ball tool below the smile. Roll a tiny piece of Terracotta-coloured MMP into a ball and push it into the mouth to give depth. For the teeth, roll a tiny sausage of White MMP and glue onto the upper part of the mouth with a little edible glue.

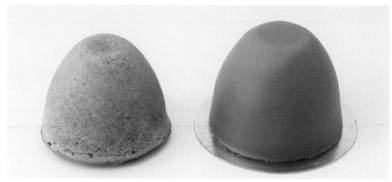

33 Make the rest of the facial features in the same way as for the grandson. Pipe dots of white royal icing onto each ear to make earrings.

34 Make the hair from MMP coloured with Bulrush and a touch of Poppy. Attach the hair to the head as explained for the grandson. Push the head down onto the cocktail stick sticking out of the body, slightly tilted to one side. To make the bun in the hair, roll a piece of the same paste into a teardrop shape, mark several lines and glue to the back of the head with a little edible glue. Finish with loose strands of hair made with thin sausages of paste and secure to the head with edible glue.

GRANNY

Body

35 Roll out 250g (8¾oz) of Terracotta sugarpaste to a thickness of 5mm (just over ⅛") on a work surface dusted with icing sugar. Place the paste carefully over the cake and smooth the paste down with the palm of your hand, pressing gently around the sides. Trim the excess paste from around the bottom of the cake using a sharp knife. Rub a smoother over the sides to achieve a neat finish.

36 To make the upper torso, roll 60g (2oz) of Poppy MMP into a ball. Glue to the top of the skirt with a little edible glue, then press the ball into it gently to flatten it down. Insert a ⅛" into the torso to support the head later and set aside.

37 Thinly roll out some Rose-coloured MMP for the collar and cut out a circle using a 3.5cm (1⅜") round cutter. Cut a 'v' on one side, then glue on top and slightly to the front of the torso. For the buttons, roll two tiny balls of Poppy MMP and glue to the front of the body. Make a hole in each button with the tip of a cocktail stick.

38 To make the apron, roll out some Sunflower-coloured MMP to a thickness of 3mm (⅛") and cut out a trapezium shape. Glue to the front of the skirt, right under the torso, with a little edible glue. Cut a strip 1cm (³⁄₈") wide from the trimmings and glue around the waist to make the apron ties. To paint the apron use Sunflower, Rose, Poppy and Holly/Ivy liquid food colours. Using a fine paintbrush, paint dots, leaves and circles in your own design all over the apron.

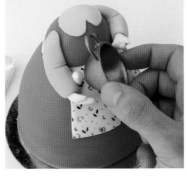

39 For the sleeves, roll some Rose-coloured MMP into a sausage and divide it in half. Make one end of each sausage slightly narrower than the other. Push a small ball tool into the wider end for the hands to be inserted into later on. Make a mark halfway along the sleeves and bend to the angle required. Glue the arms to the torso with a little edible glue.

40 Roll a small piece of Soft Beige MMP into a sausage and divide it in half for the hands. Roll each piece into a long bottle-neck shape, leaving a tiny piece of paste at the end to create the hand. Flatten the hands and cut out a 'v' shape to create a thumb. Make three marks for the fingers.

41 Glue the hands into the sleeves with a little edible glue, then glue the copper bowl to her

right arm with a dot of royal icing, and support the bowl in position until it has firmed. Finish the bottom end of the skirt with piped waves and dots of pale Terracotta-coloured royal icing.

Head

42 Roll 50g (1¾oz) of Soft Beige MMP into an oval shape. Create a smile as before then open the mouth by pushing a Dresden tool or small ball tool below the smile.

43 Using the tip of a cocktail stick, open the eye sockets along the imaginary middle line across the face. To make the bags under the eyes, press a Dresden tool sideways directly below each eye.

44 For the nose, roll a tiny piece of paste into an oval shape,

then glue just below the eyes in the middle of the face. Make the nostrils with the handle of a paintbrush.

45 To indent the cheeks, make curved lines from the sides of the nose up to the sides of the mouth and cheeks with a Dresden tool or the end of a paintbrush. Make a few marks on the smile line and forehead to create wrinkles.

46 For the ears, make a hole in each side of the head following the eye line, then roll two tiny pieces of paste into teardrop shapes and stick them into the sockets with a little edible glue. Press a small ball tool into each ear to give shape.

47 Roll a tiny piece of Terracotta paste into a ball and push it into the mouth to give depth. For the teeth, roll a tiny sausage of White MMP

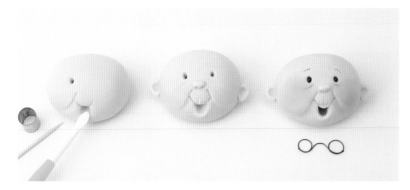

and glue onto the upper part of the mouth with a little edible glue. Dust the cheeks with Pastel Pink dust food colour.

48 Fill the eye sockets with some piped Jet Black-coloured royal icing. When dry, paint two tiny dots of Edelweiss paste food colour onto the eyes to highlight them. Paint the eyebrows and the area under her eyes with a fine paintbrush and Chestnut liquid food colour. Leave the head to firm up.

49 Make the hair at the back of her head with Cream Celebration MMP in the same way as explained for the other figures. Place the head onto the neck, tilting it slightly to one side. For the bun, roll some MMP into a sausage and emboss lines with the back of a knife. Roll into a knot and glue onto the top of the head with

a little edible glue. Make the fringe with the same paste. Pipe the earrings with white royal icing on each ear.

50 To finish, pipe Teddy Bear Brown royal icing into the bowl and stick the wooden spoon in position while the icing is still fresh.

ASSEMBLY

51 Position and glue the table onto the board by placing tiny balls of softened pastillage under each leg of the table. Glue the grandson's arms onto the top of the table. Position the rest of the items on the table and glue in place. Glue the granny onto one corner and the granddaughter onto the other side so she is looking at the cake on the table. The cake is safe to transport once all the pieces have been glued to the board.

TUTOR TIP

If you need more servings, present the whole scene on a square cake rather than a cake board.

Alfajores

"Alfajor" is the Argentinean name given to two round sweet biscuits joined together with *dulce de leche* mousse or jam (which is similar to a thick caramel toffee) and coated with dark or white chocolate.

To make these treats, sandwich two round vanilla or chocolate biscuits together with dark chocolate ganache or buttercream. You could also use *dulce de leche* if you wanted to make these the authentic Argentinean way. Let the filling

firm in the fridge for a few minutes. Using a fork to hold them, coat the sandwiched biscuits in tempered dark chocolate. Place the biscuits on a tray lined with baking parchment and leave the coating to set.

Stick a cherry made from marzipan on top while the chocolate is still wet. I used a real cherry stalk to finish the marzipan cherries but remember to remove this before the biscuits are eaten.

Originally this project was meant to include a cyclist, but as I was working on the old bicycle and the street lamp, the little story captured by these two objects was enough for me. It felt unnecessary to add any other figures and the age suggested by these two objects led me to use a greyscale colour scheme. This bicycle is not as fragile as it looks, so don't be afraid to make it!

PENNY-FARTHING

Edibles

20cm (8") round cake, filled and crumb-coated (see pages 32 to 34)

Sugarpaste/rolled fondant: 1kg (2lb 3¼oz) pale grey

SK Sugar Florist Paste (SFP)/gum paste: 150g (5¼oz) Black, 100g (3½oz) pale grey (mixture of Black and White), 50g (1¾oz) White

SK Designer Metallic Lustre Dust Food Colour: Silver

SK Liquid Food Colour: Black

SK Paste Food Colour: Black

SK Instant Mix Royal Icing: 50g (1¾oz)

Equipment

Basic equipment (see page 6)

25cm (10") cake drum/board

20cm (8") cake card

26-gauge floral wires: black (or any other colour if black is not available)

Textured rolling pin: bubbles

Piping nozzle: no. 2

15mm (⅝") width ribbon: black

High-tack craft glue

Templates (see page 188)

Wheels

1 To make the big and small wheel spokes, cut 26-gauge wire into segments as follows:

Two 9cm (3½") pieces and twelve 4.5cm (1¾") pieces for the big wheel;

Two 4cm (1½") pieces and twelve 2cm (¾") pieces for the small wheel.

Important Note

To make the wheel spokes I had to use inedible wire as it is the only way to make the bicycle look realistic and it also strengthens the whole structure. Always inform the recipient of the cake about the use of wires in models and make sure any items containing wires can be safely removed before the cake is eaten. Never insert wires directly into a cake or any part that is to be eaten.

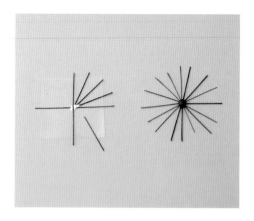

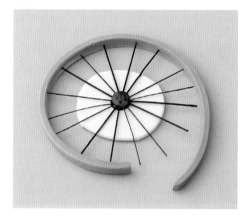

2 Build the frame on a piece of plastic sheet or thin acetate so that it can be removed easily once the glue is dry. Glue the two longer pieces of wire at right angles to each other using a drop of non-toxic glue in the centre. Glue the rest of the wire pieces in threes into each of the four sections of the cross. To glue each wire segment to the centre, dip one end into the glue and place it so that it is touching the centre in the position required.

3 Once the spoke structures of the two wheels are complete, leave the glue to dry. When it has dried, place a little royal icing into a piping bag, cut off the tip and pipe a dot onto the centre of each wheel to hide the glue and give strength to the whole structure. Allow to dry.

4 Once the icing is completely dry, peel the wheel off the plastic sheet. Paint the centre (and the wires if needed) with Black liquid food colour and allow to dry.

TUTOR TIP

Don't be tempted to pipe the centre on the other side of the wheel at this stage as it will lift the wheel and make it unstable when assembling and gluing the rest of the bicycle on a flat surface. Work on one side of the bicycle first and then, once fully dry, you can flip it over to complete the opposite side.

TYRES

5 Before making the tyres, you will need to lift the spokes a couple of millimetres from the work surface in order to build up the wheel. Thinly roll out some sugarpaste and cut out a circle smaller in size than each wheel. Push the spokes slightly down into the paste to hold them in place and to achieve the height required. Set aside.

6 To make the tyres, roll out some pale-grey coloured SFP to a thickness of approximately 3mm–4mm (1/8") and cut out a strip of 5mm (just over 1/8") in width. Lay the strip on its side and place it around the spoke frame. Push the strip of paste into the wires as you go round. To achieve a neat finish, trim the excess paste where the ends meet.

7 In order to make the wheel appear perfectly rounded, carefully fit your wheel into a round cutter of the same size and gently press the strip of paste toward the sides of cutter. Remove the cutter and set aside to dry.

MAIN FRAME

8 To make the main frame of the bicycle, roll out a strip of the grey SFP to a thickness of 3mm (1/8") and cut it to 5mm (just over 1/8") wide. Bend

over one end of the strip and trim to size following the template provided. Leave to dry on its side.

9 Thinly roll out some grey SFP and cut four narrow strips, two 4.5cm (1¾") long and two 2cm (¾") long. Allow to firm slightly then trim both pairs so that they fit between the central dot and the tyre on each wheel: these will form part of the bicycle frame. Set aside to dry completely.

HANDLEBAR

10 To make the handlebar, roll some grey SFP into a thin sausage 5cm (2") in length. Curve the sausage slightly then allow to dry. To make the support for the handle, cut a small square from the SFP and glue it to the middle of the handlebar as shown.

SADDLE

11 To make the saddle, roll some grey SFP to a thickness of 5mm (just over ⅛") and cut out a trapezium shape, following the template as a guide. Curve the saddle slightly and insert a piece of curled wire into the wider side of the seat. Set aside to dry on its side.

ASSEMBLY

12 Prepare a small paper piping bag and fill with soft-peak royal icing to glue the bicycle parts together. Stick the two wheels side-by-side then stick the main frame to the top of the big and small wheels where the paste is joined, as shown. Remove any excess icing with a fine brush.

13 Glue the thin bars of paste made earlier onto the spokes, as shown. Once these bars are in place, pipe a line of royal icing onto the side of the main frame and over the bars to join the whole structure and to make it solid. Let this side of the bicycle dry completely and then flip over and do the same on the other side. Leave it to dry again.

14 Use skewers to support the bike in an upright position on a piece of polystyrene. Roll a piece of the grey SFP into a wedge shape and use a little edible glue to stick it onto the top of the main frame where the saddle will be placed. Glue the saddle onto the wedge with a dot of royal icing.

15 Glue the handlebar in front of the seat with a dot of royal icing and remove the excess with a brush for a clean and neat finish. To add

detail, pipe a thin line of royal icing on each end of the handlebar.

16 Once the bicycle is dry, use a paintbrush to paint it with Black liquid food colour and leave to dry again.

17 To add highlights to the bicycle, use Silver metallic dust food colour diluted with a few drops of clear alcohol to paint strokes on the handlebar, the edges of the wheels and the lines of royal icing piped on the sides. Set aside to dry.

TUTOR TIP

You can make any type of bicycle following the same method to suit the recipient: just adjust the size of the wheels and the colour.

STREET LAMP

Post

18 Roll some Black SFP into a ball and push it onto a skewer that has been moistened with a little edible glue. Roll the paste and skewer on the work surface to lengthen the paste and cover the skewer. The paste should cover 15cm (6") of the skewer. Remove the excess paste from the ends and let the sausage dry upright skewered into a piece of polystyrene.

Base

19 Roll out some Black SFP to a thickness of 1cm (³/₈") and cut out two squares, one 3cm (1¹/₈") and the other 2cm (¾") in size. Glue the smaller square onto the bigger one with a little edible glue. Insert a skewer down the middle of the squares to create a hole into which the main support will be inserted later on. Set aside to dry.

20 Once dry, place the base on a piece of polystyrene and pierce the main support through the base and down into the polystyrene base. Thinly roll out a piece of paste, cut into a strip and glue to the bottom end of the post and to the base with a little edible glue. Set aside to dry.

Lamp

21 Roll out some White SFP to a 2cm (¾") thickness and make one side slightly narrower than the other by pressing a smoother onto the paste at a slight angle. Place the thinner side of the paste onto the narrower end of the lamp template, cut out the shape required and set aside to firm. Use a

skewer to make a hole through the thinner end of the lamp. Pipe lines of black royal icing onto each edge of the trapezoid lamp shape.

22 Roll out some Black SFP to a thickness of 5mm (just over ⅛") and cut out two squares for the top and bottom of the lamp; use the lamp shape as a reference to work out how big the top and bottom squares should be. Glue each square to the lamp with a little edible glue. Push the lamp through the skewer protruding from the post. Glue a strip of Black SFP between the main support and the square at the bottom of the lamp.

23 To make the top part of the lamp, roll a piece of Black SFP into a pyramid shape and glue it on top of the square. Finish by placing a tiny ball and a teardrop shape of paste on the top.

24 Once the lamp is completely dry, paint it with Silver metallic dust food colour mixed with clear alcohol, as for the bicycle.

CAKE AND BOARD

25 Roll out pale the grey sugarpaste to the size required for covering the board. Cover the board then emboss the paste with a pebble effect using a 'bubbles' textured rolling pin. Trim the excess paste from the edges and let the paste dry. Glue a length of black ribbon around the board with a non-edible glue stick.

26 Cover the cake with grey sugarpaste, then place the cake onto the board so that it is slightly off-centre. Trim the base of the cake with black ribbon.

27 Push the skewer in the lamp into one side of the cake and secure with a dot of royal icing. Place the bicycle so that it is leaning on the lamp in the required position. Use 'pebbles' of grey paste to secure the bicycle onto the cake.

WHEEL BISCUITS

These little biscuits make great little treats to go with the cake. Bake 4cm (1½")
round biscuits following the recipe provided on page 16.

Make the tyres by rolling some Black MMP to a thickness of 4mm (⅛") and
use two circle cutters of slightly different sizes to cut out a ring for each biscuit.
Attach a tyre to each biscuit with a little royal icing.

Fill a small paper piping bag with pale grey-coloured royal icing made to run-
out consistency and snip off the very tip of the bag to the size of a no. 2 round
nozzle. Flood the biscuits within the black ring and let the icing crust over.

Draw fine lines with a Black food colour pen from the centre of the biscuits to
the sides, imitating the spokes of the bicycle wheel.

Pipe a dot of royal icing in the centre, allow to dry then paint with Silver metallic
dust food colour to finish. Let the biscuits dry before wrapping them.

Moulin Rouge

When I created this character I named her Grace. With her wonderfully curvaceous figure she is ever feminine and graceful, while her showy pose and broad smile exude glamour and style. For me, Grace proves that real beauty comes in all shapes and sizes.

EDIBLES

20cm (8") round x 6cm (2³/₈") deep cake, filled and crumb-coated (see pages 32 to 34)

Sugarpaste/rolled fondant: 1.4kg (3lb 1½oz) white coloured with Cyclamen and Poinsettia (Christmas red) Paste Food Colours

SK Mexican Modelling Paste (MMP): 600g (1lb 5¼oz) Soft Beige, 180g (5¼oz) White

SK Paste Food Colours: Cyclamen, Edelweiss (white), Jet Black, Fuchsia, Poinsettia (Christmas red)

SK Professional Dust Food Colour: Cyclamen

SK Designer Pastel Dust Food Colour: Pale Peach

SK Professional Liquid Food Colour: Chestnut

SK Instant Mix Royal Icing: 50g (1¾oz)

SK CMC Gum

EQUIPMENT

Basic equipment (see page 6)

25cm (10") round cake drum/board

20cm (8") round cake card

5cm (2") diameter x 10cm (4") tall cylindrical dummy (diameter can be larger if you cannot get that size)

15mm (⁵/₈") width ribbon: burgundy

Templates (see page 188)

TUTOR TIP

This character is modelled entirely in Soft Beige MMP. It is important to use firm paste to model this figure, so add a pinch of CMC gum to the paste before you begin to achieve extra strength.

CAKE AND BOARD

1 Cover the cake with sugarpaste coloured deep red using Cyclamen and Poinsettia paste food colours (see page 34). Reserve some of the leftover paste for later then colour 200g (7oz) a deeper shade of burgundy by adding more Cyclamen paste food colour and cover the cake board (see page 37).

2 Place the cake centrally on the covered cake board. Roll a long, even sausage of sugarpaste from the trimmings and secure this around the base of the cake with edible glue.

3 Finish the edge of the board with burgundy ribbon (see page 37) and set aside to firm.

CHUBBY LEGS

TUTOR TIP

Realistic legs can be difficult to achieve when modelling a figure. Here I explain how to make them step-by-step. Follow the images and instructions carefully and with a bit of practice and patience you will be able to create curvaceous, feminine-looking legs.

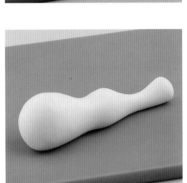

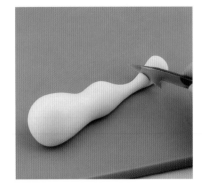

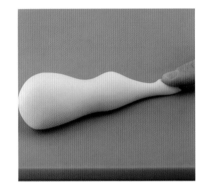

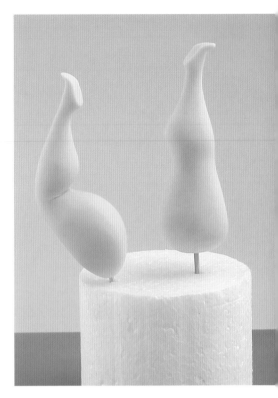

4   Roll a ball of Soft Beige MMP into a thick sausage. Press the side of your hand onto the middle, rolling the paste at the same time. This will create an indentation separating the thigh from the calf.

5   Stroke the paste on the calf side to make the ankle, leaving a piece of paste at the end to create the foot. Use a cutting tool to trim the excess paste from the foot to reduce its size if required. Use your index finger to push the paste upwards slightly towards the calf to create the heel and smooth out the sole of the foot.

6   Trim the foot at an angle and bring out the big toe. Give shape to the foot by pushing the toe down slightly and reshape the ankle if required. Gently press the back of a paintbrush halfway up the leg to bring the knee out.

7   Repeat steps 4 to 6 to make a second leg, then insert a temporary skewer greased with white vegetable fat through each thigh and up to the knee. Skewer the legs into a piece of polystyrene and allow them to dry with one leg bent and the other straight. Support the bent leg with a spare skewer if necessary until it is firm enough to hold its shape. Drying the legs in this way will prevent their sides from flattening. Once both legs have dried completely, remove the skewers.

BODY

8   Prepare a spare polystyrene cylinder of the same height as the straight leg and skewer it to a bigger polystyrene cake dummy, as shown. This will act as a temporary support to build the whole body of the character.

9   Position the legs onto the spare polystyrene cylinder and insert a cocktail stick through the top of the thighs and into the polystyrene

TUTOR TIP

This drying method applies to this figure as the legs need to be rounded and not flattened on any side. It doesn't mean that you have to use this drying method every time you model a pair of legs; it will depend on the type and shape of legs needed. For example, if the character is lying down on a flat surface you will need to leave them to dry on a flat surface without skewering them in any position.

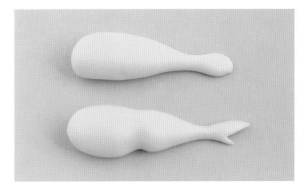
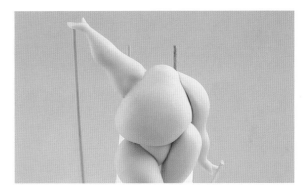

cylinder. Once the legs are in the required position glue a piece of paste between them to create the pelvis: this will give unity to the whole structure.

10 For the body, roll the paste into a rounded pear shape and glue it on top of the legs with a little edible glue. Set aside to firm up.

ARMS

11 Roll the Soft Beige paste into a thick sausage and stroke it at one end to create the wrist, leaving a small piece of paste at the end for the hand. Flatten down the hand and make a little 'v' shaped cut at one corner of the rounded end to bring out the thumb. Trim the remaining portion at an angle with a cutting tool. There's no need to indent the rest of the fingers as she will be wearing gloves.

12 Glue the arms to the sides of the torso in the position shown in the picture and rub the shoulders with your fingertips to smooth the join with the torso. Support the right arm with a skewer until it is fully dry.

HEAD

13 The head and hat are made from one piece of paste. Roll some Soft Beige MMP into a teardrop shape with a pointed end, as shown. Push a cocktail stick into the pointed end for the headdress to be inserted into later.

14 Push a small round cutter into the lower half of the ball to indent a smile then push a small ball tool underneath the smile to open up the mouth. Shape the corners of the mouth with a Dresden tool.

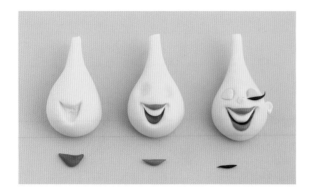

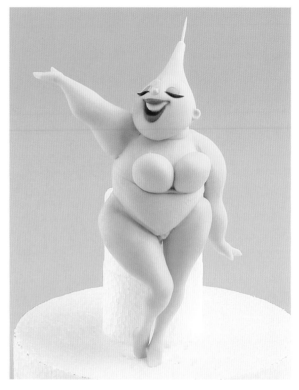

15 Roll a small piece of Cyclamen-coloured MMP into a crescent shape and fill in the mouth to give it depth. To make the upper teeth, roll some White MMP into a sausage with pointed ends and glue onto the upper part of the mouth with a little edible glue. For the lips, roll two pieces of Poinsettia-coloured MMP into sausages with pointed ends and glue them to the upper and lower parts of the mouth.

16 To make the eye sockets, push a ball tool into the paste halfway up the face. To make the eyelids, roll some Soft Beige MMP into a tiny ball, flatten it down and cut it in half to create two hemispheres. Glue each hemisphere into the eye sockets and use a paintbrush to paint them with a mix of Fuchsia and Edelweiss paste food colour. For the eyelashes, roll a tiny piece

of Jet Black-coloured MMP into a thin sausage and split it in half. Roll each piece into a sausage with pointed ends and glue to the lower part of each eyelid.

17 To make the ears, roll a tiny piece of Soft Beige MMP into a sausage and split it in half. Roll each piece of paste into an oval shape and glue to the sides of the head, following the eye-line. Press a small ball tool into the ears to shape them.

18 For the nose, roll a tiny piece of Soft Beige paste into a teardrop and glue it onto the middle of the face with the rounded end facing down. Pinch the rounded end to turn up the nose. Use a fine paintbrush and Chestnut liquid food colour to paint the eyebrows then blush the cheeks with Pale Peach dust food colour. Leave the head to firm up.

FINISHING THE BODY

19 At this point, create the stomach by adding a triangular piece of paste from the join of the thighs up to the waistline. Trim the excess paste and blend it into the body by rubbing your finger gently over the paste. Make two ball shapes for the lady's breasts and glue them above the waist with a little edible glue. Press them slightly on the lower half to shape them.

20 For the neck, roll some Soft Beige MMP into an oval shape and glue it on top of the body. Flatten the neck down slightly and skewer the head onto the neck in the required position.

COSTUME

21   To outline the costume and decorate the figure, roll pieces of White MMP into sausages and glue them on below the stomach, onto the breasts and onto the forehead line to outline the front and back of the hat. Glue another sausage around the pointed end of the hat and two thin sausages on each forearm to create the cuff of the gloves. Roll two small sausages into scrolls and glue in front of each ear.

22   To give unity to the whole piece, brush the surface of the costume, gloves and hat with soft-peak white royal icing using a medium paintbrush. Stipple the surface with the same brush to achieve a rough, uneven texture.

HEADDRESS

23   Roll small pieces of White MMP into several sausages with pointed ends. Roll them up into scrolls and leave them to firm up for a while. To build up the plume of feathers at the top, pierce one of the scrolls with a cocktail stick and, when dry, glue the rest of the scrolls of different sizes around it to give volume. Once dry, insert and glue this to the headdress with a dot of royal icing. Make fresh scrolls to cover the join of the headdress for a neat finish. Set aside to dry.

PILLAR SUPPORT AND STAIRS

24   Add a pinch of CMC gum to the sugarpaste left over from the cake covering and use this for the dummy support and the stairs.

25   Cover the top and sides of the cylindrical dummy separately. To cover the top, roll out some sugarpaste on a work surface dusted with icing sugar. Brush the top of the cylinder with some soft royal icing or edible glue and press gently onto the paste. Trim the excess paste with a cutter or sharp knife.

26   To cover the sides of the cylinder, roll out some paste and cut a strip the same height as the cylinder. Brush the surface of the paste with edible glue, place the cylinder onto one end and roll it up until the paste covers the sides completely. Trim off the excess paste with a sharp knife and set aside to dry.

27   To make the stairs, roll the remaining sugarpaste to a thickness of 5mm (just over $^1/_8$") and

cut three circles using the templates provided. Centre and glue each circle on top of each other. Glue the stairs onto a 15cm (6") diameter cake card to prevent them from sinking into the dowelled cake.

28 Secure the cylinder onto the stairs with a dab of royal icing or softened paste. Leave the support to dry completely before placing the figure on it.

29 Remove the figure from its temporary polystyrene cylinder and glue it onto the final pillar with some softened SFP. The cocktail sticks protruding from the back of each thigh (see point 9) will help support the figure in place when inserted into the final pillar.

Note: If you are using a sponge cake filled with chocolate ganache or buttercream filling, it is advisable to dowel the cake to prevent the top decoration from sinking into it. Instructions for dowelling a cake are given on page 38. (If you are using a rich fruit cake, there is no need for dowelling.) Place the figure, complete with stairs and pillar support, centrally on top of the cake.

FEATHER BOA

30 To make the boa, roll some White MMP into a sausage and place it hanging from the right arm to the back, over the left arm and down to the cake. Just leave the paste to firm up in the position required but do not glue it in place. Once dry, remove it from the body and texture it by stippling

pink royal icing (coloured with Fuchsia paste colour) all over the surface of the sausage. Once dry, dust with Cyclamen dust food colour and brush with Edelweiss paste food colour to give texture. Once finished, put the boa back in place and secure it with dots of royal icing.

TUTOR TIP

If you are transporting the cake it is safest to take the figure, boa, pillar and stairs all in one piece separately from the cake. The cake card underneath will help you lift the piece easily and will also prevent the dowels in the cake from damaging the decoration. Upon arrival at the venue, simply place the decoration (complete with cake card) onto the cake.

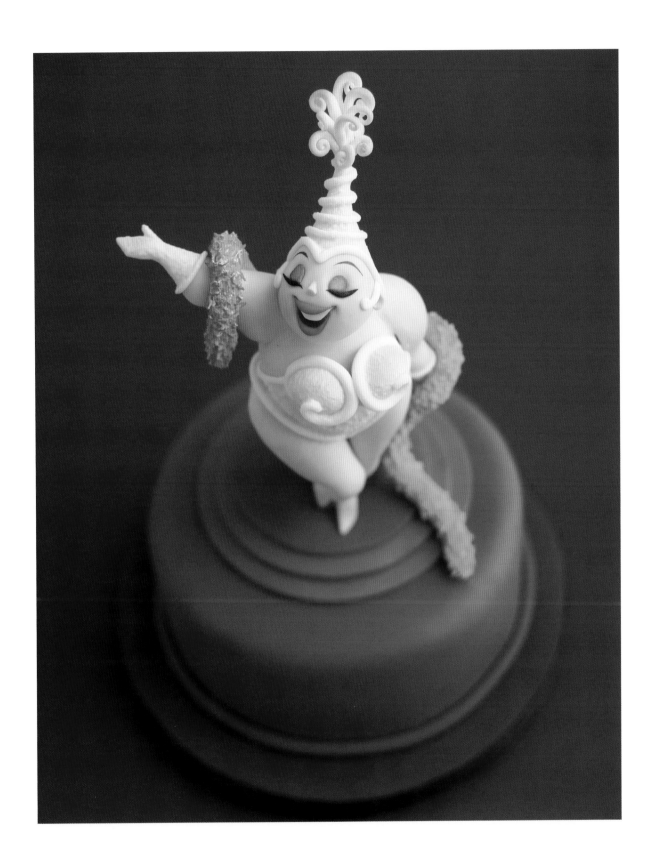

Sweet domes

Use the recipe for orange cake on pages 13 to
14 to create these mini treats for your guests.
Bake in small hemisphere silicone moulds and
coat them with liquid fondant coloured to match
the colours used in the main project. Coat them
as explained in the orange cake recipe and serve
in pretty cake cases.

JUST MARRIED

The idea of making a bride and groom for the wedding cake has been around for decades, so Elio and I really enjoyed creating a contemporary couple. We based the outfit on the actual dress and suit of the newlyweds, so you can change the outfits for the recipients. To make this wedding couple I have used a technique which I call '3D collage'. This technique is perfect for making a figure with correct proportions: simply follow the templates provided as a guide to get the length and size required for each individual piece.

Edibles

20cm (8") round cake, filled and crumb-coated (see pages 32 to 34)

Sugarpaste/rolled fondant: 1.2kg (2lb 10¼oz) white

SK Mexican Modelling Paste (MMP): 200g (7oz) Cream Celebration, 50g (1¾oz) Soft Beige, 200g (7oz) White

SK Sugar Florist Paste (SFP)/gum paste: 100g (3½oz) Black, 20g (¾oz) Cream, 20g (¾oz) Cyclamen, 20g (¾oz) White coloured with Fuchsia Paste Food Colour

SK Professional Paste Food Colours: Bulrush, Edelweiss (white), Fuchsia

SK Designer Pastel Dust Food Colour: Pastel Pink

SK Professional Liquid Food Colours: Chestnut, Poppy

SK Instant Mix Royal Icing: 50g (1¾oz) White

Equipment

Basic equipment (see page 6)

28cm (11") round cake drum/board

11cm (4½") round polystyrene dummy

Small flower cutters (Lily of the Valley or similar)

Food-grade foam pad

15mm and 25mm (⅝" and 1") width ribbon: white

7mm (¼") width ribbon: black

Templates (see page 189)

Bride

Dress

1 To make the wedding dress, roll 150g (5¼oz) of Cream Celebration MMP into a smooth ball. Roll the ball into a long cone shape and flatten it slightly with the palm of your hand. Place the shape on the template and adjust it to match the size of the dress required. Trim off the excess paste at the top and bottom of the cone using a sharp knife. Insert a skewer from the bottom to ¾ of the way up the dress.

Tutor Tip

Grease the skewer with a little vegetable fat to make it easier to insert and remove when necessary.

2 For the bodice, roll 20g (¾oz) of Cream Celebration MMP into a rounded teardrop shape and flatten it down. Trim off the excess paste at the top and bottom of the teardrop to the size required. When making the top try to match it with the depth of the skirt so both pieces will fit together neatly. To make the neckline, cut the paste into a 'v' shape using a sharp knife or a teardrop shape cutter.

3 To make the chest and neck, roll some Soft Beige MMP into a bottle shape and flatten the thicker part down. Cut out a 'v' shape to fill in the shape of the neckline. Glue the chest and neck to the top with a little edible

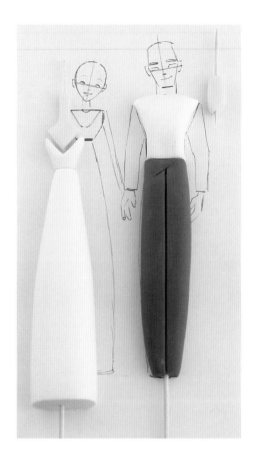

Tutor Tip

The shape of the head helps to determine the expression of the character. The rounded teardrop shape of the bride's head gives her a young, cute look. For less delicate characters, make the head into a longer, pointed teardrop.

glue, then insert a cocktail stick into the neck and torso, leaving some protruding from the neck. Set aside to firm up on a flat surface.

Head

4   For the head, roll 15g (½oz) of Soft Beige MMP into a rounded teardrop shape. To make the smile, push a small round cutter into the lower half of the paste. Roll a tiny piece of Soft Beige MMP into an oval shape for the nose and glue it above the smile.

5   Use a fine paintbrush and Chestnut liquid food colour to paint two curved lines for the eyes, halfway down the face. Paint the eyebrows above each eye with the same food colour. Paint two tiny eyelids on top of the eyes using

Chestnut liquid food colour mixed with a dot of Edelweiss paste food colour. Using a fine paintbrush, paint the lips with Poppy liquid food colour.

6   For the ears, roll two small pieces of Soft Beige MMP into ovals, glue them to the sides of the head following the eye line and press a small ball tool into each ear to give shape. Dust the cheeks with Pastel Pink dust food colour and set aside to dry.

7   For the hair, roll some Bulrush-coloured MMP into a teardrop shape and glue it to the back of the head and up to the hairline with a little edible glue. Make a few marks on the paste using a cocktail stick to create the hair strands at the front. Insert a cocktail stick into the head temporarily and leave to dry in an upright position until the hair at the back is firm.

8   Make the bun of hair by rolling a piece of the Bulrush MMP into a teardrop shape, then glue it to the back and top of the hair, pushing the paste slightly to one side. Texture with a cocktail stick. Skewer the head into a piece of polystyrene to let the hair dry without it flattening at the back.

9   Roll some Cream Celebration MMP into a sausage with pointed ends for the bride's headband and glue it over the join of the two pieces of hair from ear to ear with a little edible glue.

Assembling the body

10   Once the dress is dry enough to handle, skewer it into a piece of polystyrene. Glue the top of the dress to the skirt with softened paste and cover the join with a strip of Black SFP to make the waistband.

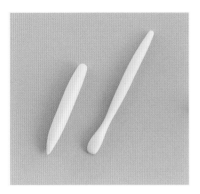

11 For the arms, roll a piece of Soft Beige MMP into a long, thin sausage and stroke one end to narrow the wrist and bring out the hand. Glue the right arm to the side of the torso and onto the front of the dress with a little edible glue. Set aside to dry.

12 To make the little flowers for the dress pattern, thinly roll out some Cream SFP onto a non-stick board greased with a little vegetable fat. Cut out several small and medium flowers with a Lily of the Valley cutter or any other similar cutter. Place the flowers on a foam pad and press a

small ball tool onto each petal of the flower to cup them. Turn each flower over and press a small ball tool into the centre then set aside to dry.

BOUQUET

13 To make the flowers in the bouquet, thinly roll out some Fuchsia and Cyclamen SFP and cut out several small flower shapes. Press them with a medium ball tool to smooth down the edges and to give shape. Set them aside to dry, leaving them slightly folded. Once dry, use royal icing to glue the flowers in a bunch on top of the right hand at the front of the dress.

14 To create the dress pattern, glue different sized cream flowers onto the front right-hand corner of the dress with dots of white

royal icing. Glue smaller flowers to the centre of medium-sized flowers to create the pattern and pipe tiny dots of royal icing between the flowers as shown. Pipe a line of white royal icing along the neckline of the dress.

15 Push the head down the cocktail stick at the neck and secure it with a dot of royal icing. Support the head with skewers in the required position until fully dry.

GROOM

Legs and body

16 For the trousers, knead 80g (2¾oz) of White MMP with a small piece of Black SFP to make a grey shade. Roll this paste into a sausage that is thinner at one end and flatten it down slightly. Place the

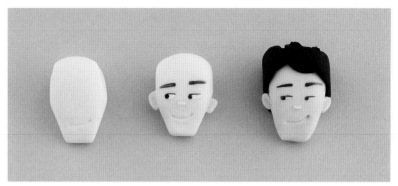

Tutor Tip

Square-shaped faces convey masculinity: start with a rounded teardrop then square off the paste around the jaw line. Adding strong features such as thick eyebrows or a big nose will add to the character's masculine look.

sausage onto the template and trim the bottom and top to size. Use the edge of a ruler to create the separation between the legs. Push a skewer into the paste from the bottom up to ⅔ of the length of the trousers.

17 For the torso, roll out 30g (1oz) of white sugarpaste to the same height as the trousers and cut out the shape required following the template. Glue to the trousers and set aside to dry on a flat surface.

18 For the neck, roll a small piece of Soft Beige MMP into a sausage that matches the template. Skewer it with a cocktail stick and glue to the torso with a little edible glue, leaving some protruding from the top. Allow the whole body to dry on a flat surface.

Head

19 To make the head, roll 15g (½oz) of Soft Beige MMP into a teardrop shape and flatten it down slightly. Place the piece of paste onto the template. Trim the paste from around the jaw line, following the template to achieve a square-shaped face.

20 Make the smile by pressing a round cutter onto the lower half of the face. Make a dimple on one corner of the smile with the tip of a cocktail stick. Roll a tiny piece of paste into an oval shape for the nose and glue it above the smile.

21 Draw the pupils halfway up the face along the eye line using a Black food colour pen. Draw a line just above each dot to make the eyelashes. Use a fine paintbrush and Edelweiss

paste food colour to paint a fine line right under the eyelashes. Use a fine paintbrush and Chestnut liquid food colour to paint the eyebrows above each eye. Make the ears and dust the cheeks as for the bride. Leave the head to dry.

22 For the hair, roll some Black SFP into a teardrop shape and glue to the back and up to the forehead with a little edible glue. Make a few marks on the paste using a cocktail stick to give texture. Insert a cocktail stick greased with white vegetable fat into the head and allow to dry in an upright position in a piece of polystyrene until the hair firms up.

23 Once the trousers, torso and neck are firm enough to handle, skewer them into a piece of polystyrene so that you can add the rest of the details easily.

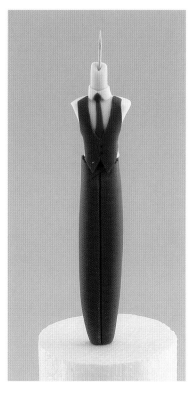

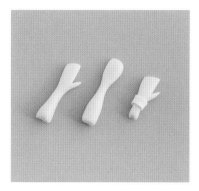

Jacket, waistcoat and tie

24 For the shirt collar, thinly roll out a little White MMP and cut out a strip approximately 1cm (³/₈") long. Glue it around the neck and trim both ends at an angle.

25 Thinly roll out some Cyclamen SFP and cut out the waistcoat using the template as a guide. Glue it to the front of the torso with a little edible glue. Draw two tiny buttons at the front with a Black food colour pen.

26 For the tie, knead a touch of Fuchsia paste food colour into the Cyclamen SFP trimmings and roll out the paste thinly. Cut out the tie shape and glue it down the middle of the torso.

27 Roll out some Black SFP and cut out the jacket following the template. Glue to the back and around the sides of the torso with a little edible glue. Notice that the jacket is longer than the torso and has to overlap at the top: bring together the paste at the top and trim the excess paste with a small pair of scissors to make a neat join at the shoulders.

28 For the lapels, thinly roll out some more Black SFP and cut out a strip, following the template. Glue it around the neck and onto the front of the jacket with a little edible glue. Glue a tiny flower onto the left lapel whilst it is still soft. Pipe dots of white royal icing onto the centre and around the little flower.

29 To make the arms, roll 20g (³/₄oz) of Black SFP into a sausage and divide it in half. Roll each piece of paste to the size of the arms following the template, then trim one end at an angle. Glue to the torso at the angled end and leave them to dry in the required position.

Tutor Tip

Position the right arm so that it is slightly away from the torso by placing a small piece of paste between the body and the arm during drying.

Hands

30 Roll 10g (¼oz) of Soft Beige MMP into a sausage and split it in half. Stroke the paste at one end to narrow the wrist, leaving a small piece of paste for the hand. Flatten the hand and cut out a 'v' shape to bring out the thumb. Trim the remaining portion of the hand at an angle then set aside to firm up.

31 Thinly roll out some White SFP and cut out two 5mm (just over 1/8") wide strips. Attach these around the wrists with a little edible glue to create the shirt cuffs. Trim off the excess paste with scissors. Stick the hands to the arms with a little edible glue.

32 To finish the groom, push the head down the cocktail stick in the neck, slightly tilted to one side. Secure in place and support as for the bride's head.

Assembly

33 To assemble the whole piece, brush the round polystyrene base with edible glue and cover with white sugarpaste in the same way as you would cover a cake (see page 38). Finish with white and black ribbon around the base then leave the paste to firm up.

34 The best way to place the figures onto the dummy cake is to insert a skewer where the bride and groom will be positioned, as shown. Remove the internal skewer from each figure then push them down onto the skewer in the dummy.

35 Once the couple is positioned on the dummy cake, make the left arm of the bride and glue it to the torso at the shoulder only. Place her hand into the groom's hand and set aside to dry. Do not glue the bride and groom's hands together if you need to transport the cake as you will need to remove the couple from the dummy and keep them separate.

Tutor Tip

I prefer to remove the skewer from each figure rather than attempt to push the figure with its skewer into the cake dummy. If the paste is not fully dry inside the figures you might tear the paste with the pressure applied when pushing the figure into the dummy, so I find this method safer. If the skewer is stuck inside the figure and cannot be removed, leave it in place then make a hole in the dummy cake with a spare skewer and insert the figure without applying too much pressure.

Mini wedding cakes

You can create these delicate variations of the main cake using the same flowers as used on the bride's dress. Simply cover the cakes as shown on page 34 and vary the size of the flowers to create two different effects. To finish, trim with a complementary narrow ribbon and present to the wedding guests in little favour boxes.

Place the couple back onto the base upon arrival at the venue.

36 Cover the cake and board with white sugarpaste (see pages 34 to 37) and place the cake centrally onto the board. Trim the cake with white and black ribbon, as for the dummy, and trim the board with white ribbon. Place the dummy, complete with the bridal couple, centrally on top of the cake.

Tutor Tip

As the cake top decoration is quite light there should be no need to dowel the cake. However, if you are worried that the cake will sink, dowel it following the instructions on page 38 before placing the dummy on top.

The original concept for this design had five different characters interacting in this winter scene, but I decided that two children having a snowball fight worked better on the cake. I really wanted to capture a sense of cheer and happiness in the children playing in a vast snowy landscape.

WINTER WONDERLAND

Edibles

12cm (5") round x 7cm (2¾") deep and 9cm (3½") round x 5cm (2") deep dome-shaped cakes (baked in dome-shaped tins, see page 11)

Sugarpaste/rolled fondant: 750g (1lb 10½oz) white

SK Mexican Modelling Paste (MMP): 100g (3½oz) Soft Beige, 370g (13oz) White

SK Paste Food Colours: Bulrush, Dark Forest, Edelweiss (white), Fuchsia, Jet Black, Lilac, Olive, Poppy, Terracotta

SK Designer Pastel Dust Food Colour: Pale Peach

SK Professional Liquid Food Colours: Blackberry, Chestnut

SK Instant Mix Royal Icing: 20g (¾oz) (optional, if used for filling the eye sockets)

Rice paper

Equipment

25cm (10") round cake drum/board

15mm (⅝") width ribbon: pale blue

Templates (see page 190)

Girl

Coat and trousers

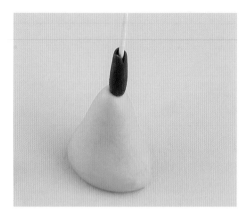

1   For the coat, colour 30g (1oz) of MMP with Fuchsia paste food colour. Save a little for the arms then roll the rest into a cone shape and insert a cocktail stick into the pointed end, leaving some protruding from the top to support the head later. For the collar, roll a small piece of Jet Black-coloured MMP into a sausage and push onto the stick.

2   To make the legs, roll a small piece of Lilac-coloured MMP into a sausage with pointed ends and cut in half. Stroke each piece of paste above the pointed end to create the ankle. Bend at the ankle and pinch to create the heel of the boots. Paint the pointed end with Blackberry liquid food colour (or Jet Black paste food colour diluted with a few drops of cooled, boiled water) to create the boots. Set aside to dry. Once the legs are firm enough to handle, glue them to the lower front of the cone in the required position with softened MMP.

3   For the arms, roll some Fuchsia-coloured MMP into a sausage with round ends and divide it in half. Bend one of the cones at a right angle and leave the other straight. Set aside to firm. Once the arms are dry, glue them to each side of the torso with softened paste, as shown. Leave to dry.

Head

4 Roll 30g (1oz) of Soft Beige MMP into a rounded teardrop shape, then push a small round cutter onto the lower half of the face to make the smile. Open up the mouth by pushing a small ball tool underneath the smile. Shape the mouth using the tip of a Dresden tool. Roll some dark Terracotta-coloured MMP into a crescent shape and push into the mouth to give it depth.

5 For the little tongue, roll a small piece of Poppy-coloured MMP into a ball and flatten it down. Glue it to the lower part of the mouth with a little edible glue. To make the front teeth, roll a small piece of White MMP into a sausage with pointed ends and glue to the upper part of the mouth. For the nose, roll a tiny piece of Soft Beige MMP into an oval shape and glue it above the mouth in the middle of the face.

6 Dust the cheeks with Pale Peach dust food colour. Use a fine paintbrush and Blackberry liquid food colour (or Jet Black paste food colour diluted with water) to paint the eyes on each side of the nose. Paint the eyebrows in the same way as for the eyes.

7 Once the face details are finished, trim the top of the head as shown using a cutter to make room for the hood later on. Set the head aside to dry.

Hood

8 To make the hood, roll some Terracotta with a touch of Poppy-coloured MMP into a rounded teardrop shape. The amount of sugarpaste used for the hood is almost the same as the amount used to make the head.

Glue it to the back of the head with the pointed end of the teardrop at the base, then ease the rounded end towards the front of the head using the palm of your hand. Push the head with the hood onto the cocktail stick protruding from the neck and position as required. Allow to firm up.

9 To make the fur trim, roll some White MMP into a sausage with pointed ends and glue it around the hood with a little edible glue. Trim the excess paste at the chin if needed. Roll another piece of White MMP into a sausage and glue it around the bottom edge of the coat.

10 To make the cuffs, roll two small balls of White MMP and glue them to the arms. Open a hole in each cuff using the handle of a paintbrush. The gloves will be inserted into these holes in the next step.

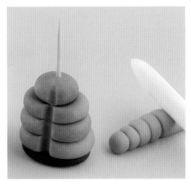

11   For the gloves, roll a small piece of Lilac-coloured MMP into a sausage and divide it in half. Roll each piece into a teardrop shape and push the back of a knife onto the rounded end to bring the thumb out. Glue them to the cuffs at the pointed end with a little edible glue and position as shown.

BOY

Legs and body

12   To make the legs, roll 40g (1½oz) of Dark Forest-coloured MMP into a long sausage with tapered ends and fold it in half. Bend the legs in half again, bringing the rounded end towards the pointed ends to create a kneeling position. For the shoes, roll two pieces of Jet Black-coloured MMP into small teardrops and glue them to the pointed ends of the legs with a little edible glue. Set aside to dry.

13   For the torso, colour 30g (1oz) of White MMP with Olive paste food colour and reserve a third of the paste for the arms. Roll the remainder into a thick sausage and make several marks along it with the side of a modelling tool or the back of the knife. Press the tool and roll the sausage at the same time to give shape to the winter jacket. Try to leave a thinner end so that you can create the collar of the jacket all in one piece. To make the trim of the jacket, roll a ball of Jet Black-coloured MMP, flatten it down and glue to bottom of the jacket.

14   To create the zip, push the back of a paintbrush into the front of the jacket to make an indentation. Roll a small sausage of black paste and glue it to the indentation. Insert a cocktail stick into the collar of the jacket to support the head later and set aside to dry.

15   Once the torso and legs are finished, glue them together with a little softened paste. For the sleeves, roll the remaining Olive-coloured MMP into a sausage and make marks as for the jacket. Trim the excess paste to the length needed and glue them to the side of the torso with a little softened paste in the required position. Set aside to dry.

Head

16   Make the head, mouth and nose as for the girl's head. Open the eye sockets by pushing the tip of a cocktail stick into the paste, then fill them with black-coloured royal icing.

Use a fine paintbrush and Edelweiss paste food colour to paint a white dot on each eye.

TUTOR TIP

If preferred you can draw the eyes instead using a Black Food Colour Pen, then paint a white dot to highlight them.

17 For the ears, roll two pieces of Soft Beige MMP into small balls and glue them onto each side of the head. Push a small ball tool into them to give shape. Paint the eyebrows and dust the cheeks as for the girl. Once the head is finished, trim the top off and set aside to dry.

18 To make the hair, colour a small piece of MMP with Bulrush paste colour, then roll the paste into a teardrop shape and use edible glue to attach it to the back of the head with the pointed end facing down. Trim away any excess paste and keep the trimmings.

19 To make the hat, roll a ball of Dark Forest-coloured MMP into a dome shape. Push the hard bristles of a brush all over the hemisphere to give a woollen texture and glue it to the top of the head. Push the head down onto the cocktail stick at the neck. Let the hat firm up before adding the rest of details.

20 To finish off the woolly hat, roll out a little Olive-coloured MMP and cut out a strip. Texture the paste as

for the hat and glue it around the hat and head, trimming the excess paste at the back. Make several marks along the paste with the blade of a knife. To make the pompom, roll some paste into a ball, texture with the brush and glue it onto the top of the hat. Add a few strands of hair in front of each ear.

21 Make the gloves as for the girl using Jet Black-coloured MMP. Glue them in the required position, as shown.

CAKE

22 Place the two cake domes towards the back of the round cake board. Secure them in place with a little buttercream then crumb-coat

the cakes with buttercream. Add a few pieces of sugarpaste on each side of the cakes to create slopes.

23 Roll out the white sugarpaste and cover the cakes and board in one piece. Smooth the paste down with the palm of your hands and trim the excess paste from the edges of the board using a sharp knife. Make a few marks on the paste while it is still soft to give the snow texture as shown. Glue a length of ribbon around the side of the board to give a neat finish.

TREES

24 To make the trees, draw them on a piece of rice paper using the template provided then cut out with

scissors. Glue them to the back of the slopes with a dot of white royal icing.

25 Place the boy and girl in the required positions and secure them with a dot of white royal icing or softened sugarpaste. Make a few snowballs with white sugarpaste, then glue them to the boy's glove and around the girl as desired to complete the winter scene.

TUTOR TIP

Where you have used inedible supports such as cocktail sticks in models, make sure you inform the recipient before the cake is served so that they can be removed safely.

Marshmallow snowballs

Follow the recipe for marshmallow on page 23 then pipe the vanilla
marshmallow into small dome-shaped silicone moulds. Sprinkle
grated coconut on top while the marshmallow is still wet and push
a plastic lolly stick into the centre of each. Once the marshmallow
has set, push each silicone dome from underneath to release the
marshmallow from the mould.

Toss each ball in grated coconut to add texture and they are
ready to eat! Try to make them a day in advance to prevent the
marshmallow from drying out and to keep them as soft as possible.

SANTA CLAUS IS ON HIS WAY!

By the magical light of the Christmas Star, Santa brings boxes of joy to us all on Christmas Day.

EDIBLES

7cm (2¾") round x 6cm (2³⁄₈") deep cake

10cm (4") round x 10cm (4") deep cake

15cm (6") round x 10cm (4") deep cake

1.2kg (2lb) marzipan (optional)

Clear alcohol (if using marzipan)

Sugarpaste/rolled fondant:

For the base tier: 350g (12¼oz) white coloured with Dark Forest Paste Food Colour, 350g (12¼oz) white coloured with Olive Paste Food Colour

For the middle tier: 450g (1lb) white

For the top tier: 50g (1¾oz) white, 50g (1¾oz) white coloured with Hydrangea Paste Food Colour, 150g (5¼oz) white coloured with Olive Paste Food Colour

For the board: 350g (12¼oz) white

SK Mexican Modelling Paste (MMP): 60g (2oz) Soft Beige, 30g (1oz) White, 60g (2oz) White coloured with Poinsettia

SK Sugar Florist Paste (SFP)/gum paste: 50g (1¾oz) White coloured with Dark Forest, 30g (1oz) White, 30g (1oz) White coloured with Poppy, 50g (1¾oz) White coloured with Sunny Lime

100g (3½oz) SK Instant Mix Pastillage

SK Paste Food Colours: Dark Forest, Holly/Ivy, Hydrangea, Jet Black, Olive, Poppy, Sunny Lime

SK Designer Metallic Lustre Dust Food Colour: Antique Gold

50g (1¾oz) SK Instant Mix Royal Icing

EQUIPMENT

Basic equipment (see page 6)

28cm (11") square cake drum/board

2 x 23cm (9") round or square spare cake drums/boards

7cm, 10cm and 15cm (2¾", 4" and 6") round cake cards

Small Lily of the Valley flower cutter

Small daisy cutter

Small leaf cutter

15mm (⁵⁄₈") width ribbon: dark green

Template for star (see page 190)

CAKE BOARD

1 Roll out 350g (1lb 2¼oz) of white sugarpaste to a thickness of 3mm–4mm (approximately ⅛") and cover the cake drum. Rub a smoother over the paste to remove any imperfections then trim the excess paste from the edges with a plain-bladed knife.

2 To add texture to the board, dilute some Holly/Ivy paste food colour with a few drops of cooled, boiled water and use a toothbrush to flick the colour onto the board using the 'splashing technique' as described on page 47. Allow to dry.

3 Glue a length of dark green ribbon onto the edge of the board with a non-toxic glue stick. Set aside to dry.

SANTA

Body and head

4 To make the body, roll 20g (¾oz) of Poinsettia-coloured MMP into a teardrop shape and insert a piece of dried spaghetti into the pointed end, leaving some protruding from the top.

5 For the head, roll 20g (¾oz) of Soft Beige MMP into a ball and push it onto the spaghetti in the body.

6 To make the belt, roll a thin sausage of White MMP and glue this around the lower half of the body at a slight angle. Make two holes at

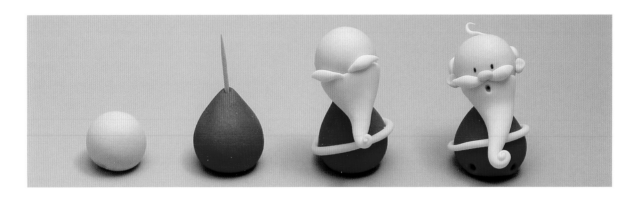

the bottom end of the body into which the legs will be inserted later on. Set aside to firm.

7 To make the beard, roll some White MMP into a cone and glue the wide end to the lower half of the head with edible glue. For the moustache, roll two small pieces of White MMP into sausages with pointed ends and glue them above the beard. Open up the mouth with a cocktail stick between the moustache and the beard.

8 For the nose, roll a small piece of Soft Beige MMP into an oval and glue it in the middle of the moustache. For the ears, roll two tiny pieces of Soft Beige MMP into balls and glue to the sides of the head, following the eye line. Press a small ball tool into them to give them shape.

9 To make the hair, roll some White MMP into a sausage shape and glue it to the back of the head from ear to ear, pressing gently to flatten the sausage down. Roll more White MMP into a tiny sausage with pointed ends and glue this to the head to make the curled tuft of hair.

10 Draw on the eyes using a fine Black food colour pen. To create the light in the eyes, dip the tip of a cocktail stick into Edelweiss paste food colour and gently touch each eye, leaving a tiny dot on them. To make the eyebrows, roll two small pieces of White MMP into teardrop shapes and glue them above each eye.

LEGS AND SHOES

11 Make the legs and shoes in one piece. Roll a thin sausage of White SFP with one long, pointed end. Curl the pointed end up to make the scroll as shown. Pinch the curved side to make a right angle and bring the heel out. Make two and leave to dry completely.

12 Once dry, use a fine paintbrush to paint the shoe with Jet Black paste food colour diluted with a few drops of cooled, boiled water, then paint two red strips with diluted Poppy paste food colour on the remaining portion to make the stocking. Set aside to dry.

13 Push the legs into the holes in the lower half of the body and secure with a little edible glue.

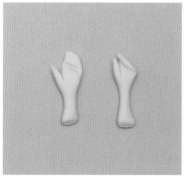

ARMS AND HANDS

14 Roll a small piece of Soft Beige MMP into a sausage shape and split in half. Roll each piece into a long bottleneck shape to form a wrist, leaving a tiny piece of paste at the end to create the hand. Flatten the hands and cut a 'v' shape out of each to create a thumb. Trim the remaining portion at an angle to shape the hand. In order to bend the fingers on the right hand, make a mark with a cocktail stick and bend along this mark. Leave the hands to dry.

15 For the sleeves, roll some Poppy-coloured MMP into a sausage and divide it in half. Make one end of each piece slightly narrower than the other then bend the right arm at an angle. To keep the left arm upright without it falling off, insert a piece of dried spaghetti into the narrower end of

the sleeve and into the body, then glue the arm to the body with a little edible glue. Glue the bent arm to the torso, making sure you line up the narrower end with the top of the torso.

16 To make the white cuffs, roll two small balls of White MMP and glue to the wider end of each sleeve. Press the handle of a brush into this end of the arms to open up a hole for the hands. To insert the hands, trim the excess paste at the wrist at an angle, push gently into the socket and place them in the required position. Secure the hands in place with a little edible glue.

STAR

17 Thinly roll a small piece of pastillage and cut out a star shape using the template provided. Leave it to dry on a flat surface.

18 Once dry, paint the star with Antique Gold dust food colour mixed with a few drops of clear alcohol. Paint a piece of dried spaghetti with diluted Jet Black paste food colour and stick it to the back of the star with royal icing. Set aside to dry. Once dry, insert the spaghetti into the straight sleeve, which should now be firm.

RIBBONS

19 For the curled ribbons, thinly roll out the Sunny Lime-coloured SFP onto a non-stick board greased with a little vegetable fat and

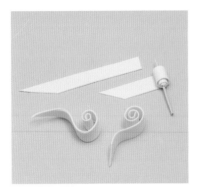

cut out strips 1cm (³/₈") wide using a large, sharp knife to make a neat cut. Trim one end of the strip at an angle and leave the other end straight. Roll up the strip starting at the straight end, using a cocktail stick to help you roll the paste tightly. Remove the cocktail stick and lay the strip on its side to allow the curl to loosen. Leave to dry.

20 To make the ribbon loops, cut out strips of Dark Forest SFP 1.5cm (½") and 2cm (¾") wide with straight ends. Brush a little edible

glue on the ends of the strips and press them together. Leave the strips to dry on their side. Cut spare strips of paste, lay them on their side and make wavy shapes. Leave all the ribbon pieces to dry.

PASTILLAGE WEDGES

21 Roll out some pastillage to a thickness of 1cm (³/₈"). Press a cake smoother at an angle on one side of the paste to make it thinner, then cut out circles using 8cm (3¹/₈") and 5cm (2") round cutters.

COVERING THE CAKES

22 If you wish to cover all three cakes with a layer of marzipan first, follow the technique for covering cakes with straight edges as explained on page 36 and then cover with sugarpaste as described below. If you are using sponge cakes and you do not want to use marzipan, omit this step and continue to cover the cakes as described below. Turn the cakes upside-down on a spare board and crumb-coat with a layer of buttercream so that the sugarpaste will stick onto the cake.

BASE TIER

23 To create a marbled effect, knead 350g (12¼oz) of Dark Forest sugarpaste and 300g (12¼oz) of Olive sugarpaste together until streaky. Roll the paste into a sausage shape, then roll this out into a long rectangle on a work surface dusted with icing sugar. The rectangle of paste should be the same height as the cake and long enough to place around the cake that is to be covered: use a paper template to measure the circumference of your cake if needed.

24 To stick the paste onto the cake, roll up the marbled strip, lay the roll on its side next to the cake then unroll the strip around the cake while pressing gently with the palm of your hand. Bring the ends together then trim the excess paste at the join and smooth with a cake smoother. At this point, use a toothbrush to splash the paste with diluted Holly/Ivy paste food colour in the same way as for the board.

25 Knead the trimmings of paste together until the colours are completely blended. Roll out the paste into a long strip that is 3mm (¹/₈") thick and cut out a strip 2cm (¾") wide. Brush a little edible glue along the middle of the strip and place around the bottom of the cake to create the side of the lid. Match the ends with the join in the cake covering. Leave the paste to firm for a few hours.

26 Once the sugarpaste has firmed, turn the cake back round the right way, using a cake board to help you flip the cake over.

27 Spread some buttercream on top of the cake (or brush with clear alcohol if you have used marzipan). Roll out the remaining paste into a circle slightly bigger than the diameter of the cake that is to be covered to a thickness of 3mm (¹/₈"). Centre the sugarpaste circle onto the cake, place the spare cake drum gently back on top and flip the cake over again. Trim the excess paste from the edge using a sharp knife, following the side of the cake as a guide.

28 Turn the cake back round the right way and allow the paste covering to firm. Once the cake is finished, place it onto the covered board, making sure you use the cake card underneath to lift it. Secure the cake onto the board with royal icing.

29 To decorate the side of the cake, cut several small daisies from White SFP, then add Sunny Lime-coloured centres and small Dark Forest-coloured leaves, all made from

 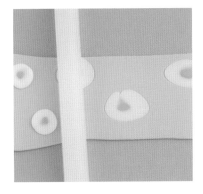 

SFP. Glue them to the side of the cake with a little edible glue, creating a pattern of your choice.

MIDDLE TIER

30 Cover the second tier with white sugarpaste, following the same method as explained for the first tier. To decorate the sides of the cake, thinly roll out the Poppy-coloured SFP and cut out several flowers using a small Lily of the Valley cutter. Use a ball tool to smooth the edges and give shape. Leave some of the flowers in one piece and trim some into two- or three-petal flowers. Glue them to the sides of the cake (excluding the lid) with a little edible glue, then pipe small dots of Jet Black-coloured royal icing using a paper piping bag to create a pattern.

TOP TIER

31 To create the pattern on the top tier, roll out 30g (1oz) of white sugarpaste into a rectangle. Next, roll some Hydrangea-coloured sugarpaste into a sausage and glue the white paste around it with a little edible glue. Trim off the excess paste and roll the sausage gently to smooth out the join. Cut pieces 5mm (just over 1/8"") thick out of the roll. Roll out a strip of Olive-coloured sugarpaste big enough to cover the sides of the small cake then place the pieces of the roll onto the strip of sugarpaste. Roll over the paste with a rolling pin to flatten and join the pastes together, trim to size and cover the side of the cake as explained above.

32 Make the lid as before from Olive-coloured sugarpaste and allow to firm.

ASSEMBLY

33 Before stacking the cakes, dowel the base tier following the instructions on page 38, ensuring that the dowels fit within the diameter of the pastillage wedge. Centre the first tier on the board, gluing it with a dot of royal icing. Once the cake has been dowelled, attach the 8cm (3¹/₈") pastillage wedge to the cake with a dab of royal icing.

34 Use royal icing to stick the middle tier onto the pastillage wedge. Dowel the middle tier with one plastic dowel where the pastillage base will be positioned. (One dowel is enough as the third tier is quite small and light.) Secure with royal icing as for the lower tiers.

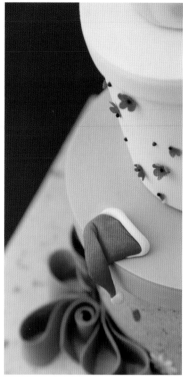

FINISHING TOUCHES

35 Arrange the ribbons on the board and the middle tier in any way you like, gluing them together and onto the cake with dots of royal icing.

36 Model Santa's hat with a cone of Poppy MMP. Add a thin sausage of White MMP for the brim and a pompom on the top. Glue onto the edge of the base tier with edible glue.

TUTOR TIP

This cake can usually be transported in one piece as it is not too big. However, if you find that the crooked cake is too difficult to transport, just stack the cakes on top of each other in the traditional way. Another way to achieve a crooked effect for the cake without using pastillage wedges is to make the round cakes slightly slanted before you cover them with sugarpaste.

CHRISTMAS MINI CAKES

These mini cakes make lovely little gifts and are a great way to use up the flowers, stars and curled ribbons left over from the main project. I have chosen to cover them with different tones of the same olive green hue to create a warm colour scheme, but of course you can make them in any colour you wish.

Place each cake on a cake card then cover them with sugarpaste following the instructions on page 34. Trim with ribbon then attach your chosen decoration using dots of royal icing.

TEMPLATES

Queen of Hearts, pages 65–72

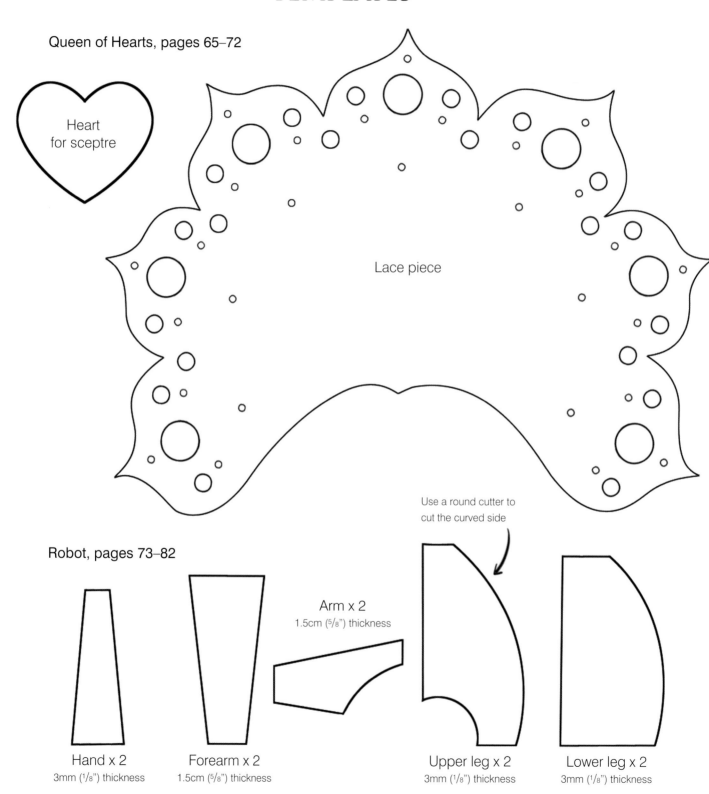

Heart
for sceptre

Lace piece

Use a round cutter to
cut the curved side

Robot, pages 73–82

Arm x 2
1.5cm (⁵⁄₈") thickness

Hand x 2
3mm (¹⁄₈") thickness

Forearm x 2
1.5cm (⁵⁄₈") thickness

Upper leg x 2
3mm (¹⁄₈") thickness

Lower leg x 2
3mm (¹⁄₈") thickness

Robot, pages 73–82

The Quest for Food,
pages 93–102

Pasillage cup 3mm (¹/₈") thickness

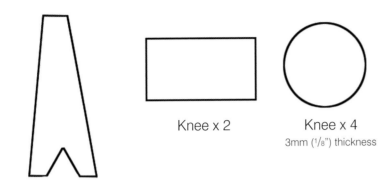

Knee x 2

Knee x 4
3mm (¹/₈") thickness

Foot x 2
1.5cm (⁵/₈") thickness

Hips x 1 5mm (just over ¹/₈") thickness

Flora the Woodland Fairy,
pages 83-92

The Quest for Food,
pages 93–102

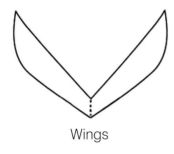

Wings

Cup handle

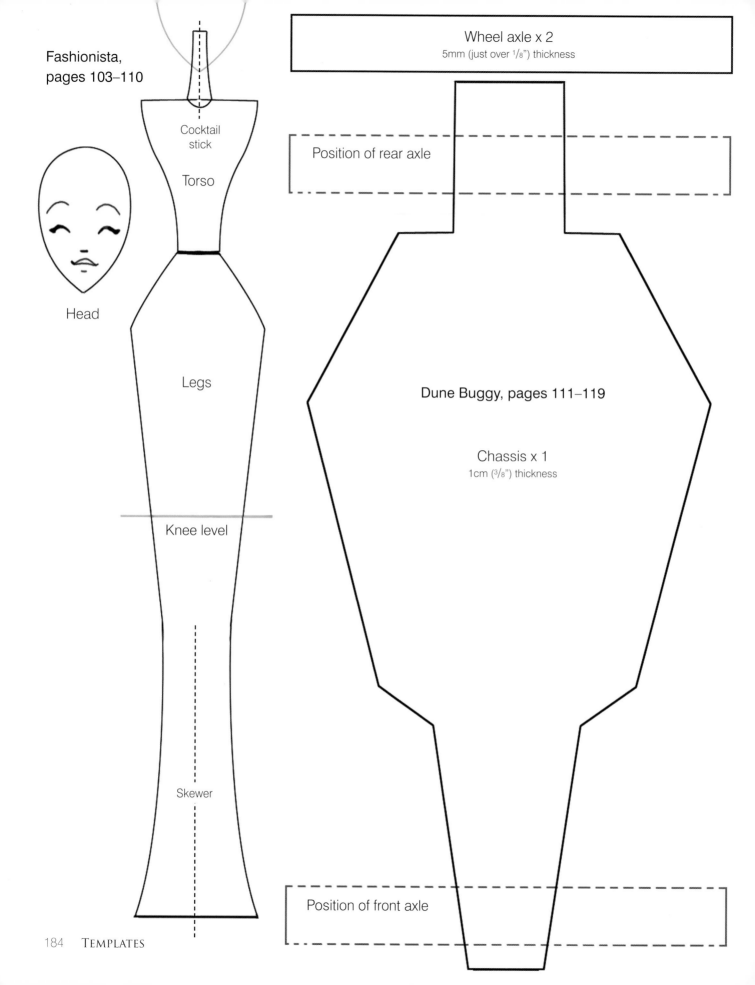

Fashionista,
pages 103–110

Head

Cocktail
stick

Torso

Legs

Knee level

Skewer

Wheel axle x 2
5mm (just over 1/8") thickness

Position of rear axle

Dune Buggy, pages 111–119

Chassis x 1
1cm (3/8") thickness

Position of front axle

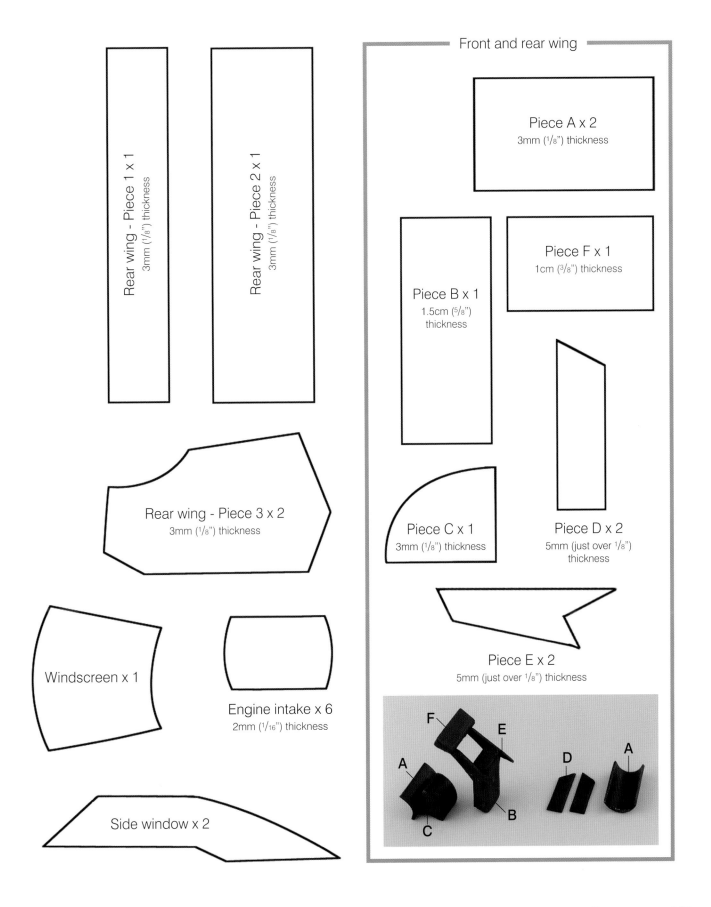

Rear wing - Piece 1 x 1
3mm (1/8") thickness

Rear wing - Piece 2 x 1
3mm (1/8") thickness

Front and rear wing

Piece A x 2
3mm (1/8") thickness

Piece B x 1
1.5cm (5/8") thickness

Piece F x 1
1cm (3/8") thickness

Rear wing - Piece 3 x 2
3mm (1/8") thickness

Piece C x 1
3mm (1/8") thickness

Piece D x 2
5mm (just over 1/8") thickness

Windscreen x 1

Engine intake x 6
2mm (1/16") thickness

Piece E x 2
5mm (just over 1/8") thickness

Side window x 2

A B C D E F
G H I J K L
M N O P Q R
S T U V W X
Y Z

Dune Buggy, pages 111–119

Letters and numbers for Dune Buggy

1 2 3 4 5 6
7 8 9 0

Granny's Kitchen,
pages 120–134

Dune Buggy, pages 111–119

Wheel rim x 4
5mm (just over 1/8") thickness

Chair
seat x 1
5mm (just over 1/8")
thickness

Chair upper front beam x 2
3mm (1/8") thickness

Chair upper side beam x 2
3mm (1/8") thickness

Chair lower beams x 2
3mm (1/8") thickness

Chair back x 1
3mm (1/8") thickness

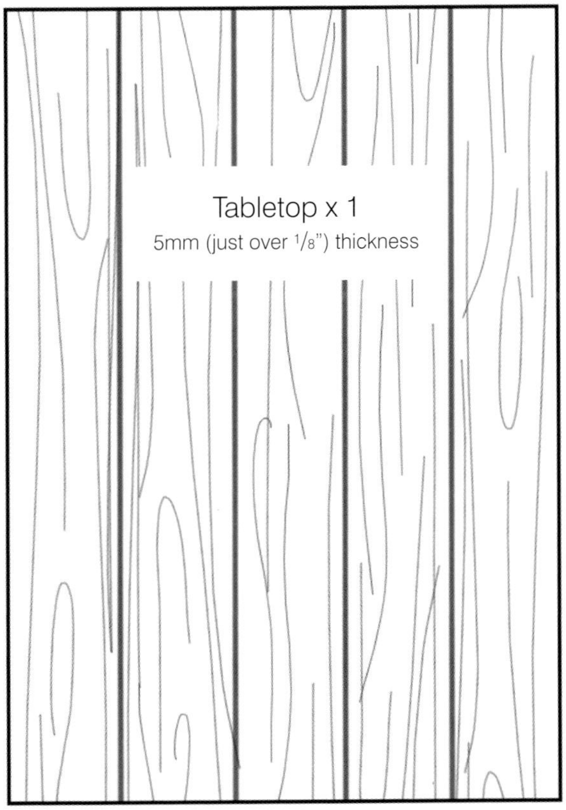

Chair back leg x 2 5mm (just over 1/8") thickness

Chair front leg x 2 5mm (just over 1/8") thickness

Tabletop x 1
5mm (just over 1/8") thickness

Table long beam x 2 5mm (just over 1/8") thickness

Table leg x 4 1cm (3/8") thickness

Table short beam x 2 5mm (just over 1/8") thickness

Table drawer x 1
3mm (1/8") thickness

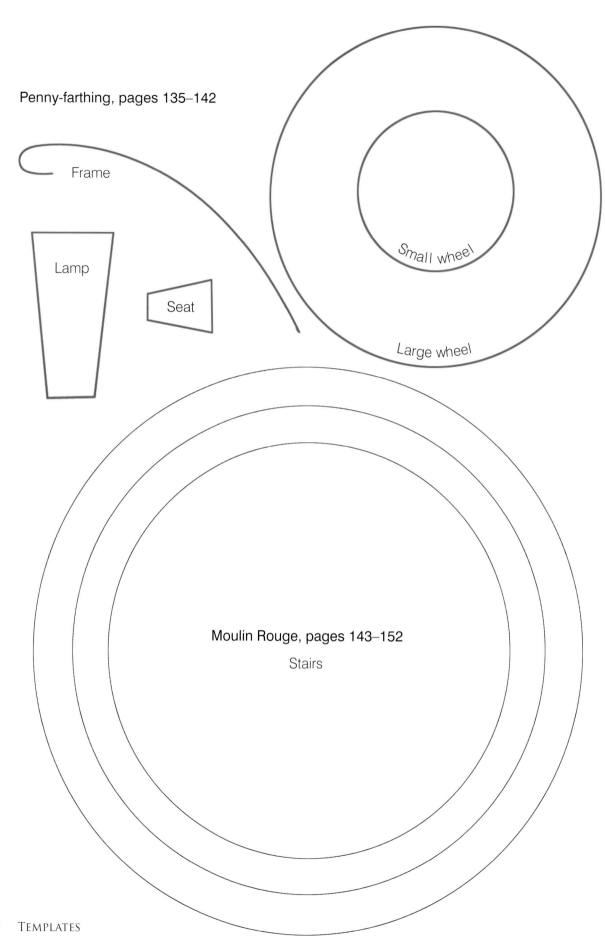

Penny-farthing, pages 135–142

Frame

Lamp

Seat

Small wheel

Large wheel

Moulin Rouge, pages 143–152

Stairs

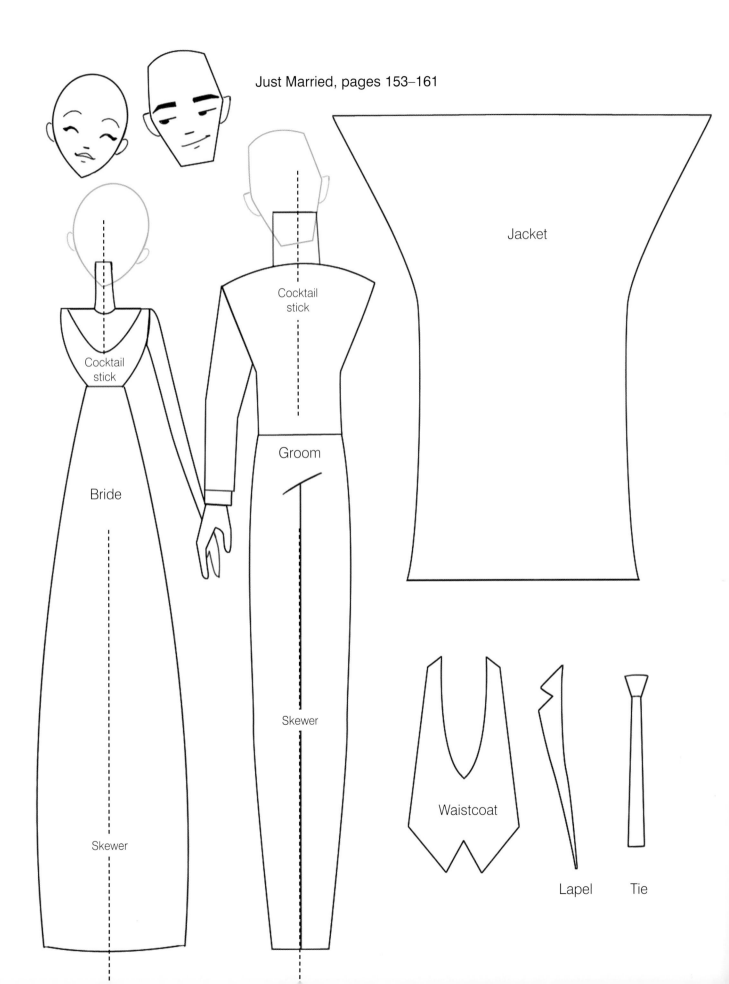

Just Married, pages 153–161

Jacket

Cocktail
stick

Cocktail
stick

Groom

Bride

Skewer

Skewer

Waistcoat

Lapel   Tie

Winter Wonderland,
pages 162–170

Trees

Santa Claus is on his Way!
Pages 171–181

Star for wand

SUPPLIERS

Squires Kitchen, UK
3 Waverley Lane
Farnham
Surrey
GU9 8BB
0845 61 71 810
+44 1252 260 260
www.squires-shop.com

Squires Kitchen International School
The Grange
Hones Yard
Farnham
Surrey
GU9 8BB
0845 61 71 812
+44 1252 260262
www.squires-school.co.uk

Squires Kitchen, France
+33 (0) 1 82 88 01 66
clientele@squires-shop.fr
www.squires-shop.fr

Squires Kitchen, Italy
www.squires-shop.it

Squires Kitchen, Spain
+34 93 180 7382
cliente@squires-shop.es
www.squires-shop.es

Stockists
UK

Jane Asher Party Cakes
London
020 7584 6177

Blue Ribbons
Surrey
020 8941 1591

Lawsons Ltd.
Devon
01752 892543

The Sugarcraft Emporium
Worcestershire
01527 576703

Surbiton Art & Sugarcraft
Surrey
020 8391 4664

SK Distributors
UK

Confectionery Supplies
Herefordshire
www.confectionerysupplies.co.uk

Guy Paul & Co. Ltd.
Buckinghamshire
www.guypaul.co.uk

Culpitt Ltd.
Northumberland
www.culpitt.com

Australia & New Zealand

Zoratto Enterprises
New South Wales
+61 (2) 9457 0009

Sweden

Tårtdecor
Kungälv
www.tartdecor.se

Manufacturers

Smeg UK Ltd.
www.smeguk.com
www.smeg50style.co.uk

Italian appliance manufacturer
Smeg produces distinctive domestic
appliances combining design,
performance and quality.